Contents

KU-484-407

Books are to be returned on or before
the last date below.

7 – DAY
LOAN

LIVERPOOL
JOHN MOORES UNIVERSITY
I.M. MARSH LRC
Tel: 0151 231 5216

WITHDRAWN

™ Nelson Thornes
(luwer business)

LIVERPOOL JMU LIBRARY

3 1111 01239 3185

LIVERPOOL
JOHN MOORES UNIVERSITY

I.M. MARSH LRC
Tel: 0151 231 5216

Text © Robert Fisher 1995, 2005
Original illustrations © Nelson Thornes Ltd 1995, 2005

The right of Robert Fisher to be identified as author of this work has been asserted by him in accordance with the Copyright, Designs and Patents Act 1988.

All rights reserved. No part of this publication may be reproduced or transmitted in any form or by any means, electronic or mechanical, including photocopy, recording or any information storage and retrieval system, without permission in writing from the publisher or under licence from the Copyright Licensing Agency Limited, of Saffron House, 6-10 Kirby Street, London EC1N 8TS.

Any person who commits any unauthorised act in relation to this publication may be liable to criminal prosecution and civil claims for damages.

First published in 1995 by:
Stanley Thornes (Publishers) Ltd

This edition published in 2005 by:
Nelson Thornes Ltd
Delta Place
27 Bath Road
CHELTENHAM
GL53 7TH
United Kingdom

07 08 09 / 10 9 8 7 6 5 4

A catalogue record for this book is available from the British Library

ISBN 978-0-7487-9442-3

Page make-up by Northern Phototypesetting Co. Ltd, Bolton

Cover photograph: Image 100 EE (NT)

Printed and bound in Spain by GraphyCems

Acknowledgements

The author wishes to thank the children and teachers who have contributed to the research for this book and in particular to Lizann O'Conor and Julie Winyard for valuable suggestions on ways to improve the second edition of this book.

Thanks are also due to the following for their generous permission to use the following material: Excerpt from 'The Road Not Taken' from THE POETRY OF ROBERT FROST edited by Edward Connery Lathem. Copyright © 1969 by Henry Holt and Company; 'What is the mystery of the funny question mark ...?' from *Curriculum for Able Children* (ed) L. Jones 1993 published by the National Association for Able Children in Education (NACE); John Manwaring's writing taken by permission from *Poetic Writing in the Primary School* by Pie Corbett (1992) published by Kent Reading and Language Development Centre.

Every effort has been made to contact the copyright holders but if any have been overlooked, the publishers will be pleased to make the necessary arrangement at the first opportunity.

Introduction

I am still learning.
    Michaelangelo

To really learn you need others to help you.
    Jody, aged 9

All human beings have a basic right to the full development of their minds and of their capacity for learning. There is a growing realisation that the development of individuals and of communities depends on education, and on the quality of teaching and learning. The needs of individuals and the needs of society meet in the need to develop lifelong and autonomous learners, students who value learning as an empowering activity, who want to learn independently and who have self-determination, self-direction and self-respect. We need to develop students who can effectively participate in society and meet the challenge of rapid social change. For teachers the challenge is – how do we foster the learning that will help achieve these goals?

In recent years, there has been a worldwide explosion of interest in ways of developing thinking and learning. Research in and development of cognitive education is progressing rapidly in many countries. This book does not set out to be a comprehensive review of all the research into teaching children to learn. Rather it is intended to serve as a practical guide to ways of teaching that have been shown to develop effective learning.

Successful learners not only have a lot of knowledge, they have also learnt how to learn. Research shows that certain teaching strategies are common to classrooms where effective learning takes place. We are now better able to identify what learners need to help them learn wisely and well.

This book describes 10 simple but powerful teaching strategies most closely linked to success in learning. These strategies can be applied to any area of learning, and are the processes most likely to achieve the goals of independent and effective learning. The 10 teaching strategies that make up the chapters of this book aim to foster the expansion of thinking and learning throughout the curriculum. These are:

1 **Thinking to learn:** *What do you think?*
    Learning is best developed through a 'thinking skills' approach, which aims to teach children not only what to learn but how to learn. This means offering challenge to thinking, and giving time for thinking, to students in all areas of their learning.

2 **Questioning to learn:** *What questions are there?*
    A characteristic of effective learners is that they ask questions – of themselves and of others. An enquiring classroom will generate questions and encourage students to develop their own questions.

3 **Planning to learn:** *What is the plan?*
    Research shows that those successful in any field tend to spend more time at the planning stage. For children, this means they need to know the value of planning, the skills of planning and to develop dispositions to follow a 'plan–do–review' process of learning.

4 **Talking to learn:** *What should we discuss?*
Children need to articulate their thinking and learning. Good teachers encourage interpretative discussion. They utilise 'think–pair–share', allowing individual thinking time, discussion with a partner, and then group or class discussion, creating in the classroom a community of enquiry.

5 **Visual tools for learning:** *Can we show what we think?*
Concept mapping (also called mind mapping) helps children to articulate their thinking, converting the verbal into the visually memorable. Mapping helps children organise what they know, and to create new patterns of understanding.

6 **Creativity and learning:** *How can we improve it?*
All learning should allow for some personal expression and individual variation. We value what we have made our own. Teaching for creativity means offering choices, encouraging individual responsibility and a creative response to learning.

7 **Collaborative learning:** *Who can help us?*
Learning with a partner or with a group can extend opportunities both for learning from and for teaching others. Children can benefit from co-operative learning with less able, more able and similar-ability peers.

8 **Coaching learning:** *What help do we need?*
Children need help to fulfil their potential as thinkers and learners. They need help through instruction and explanation but also through cognitive coaching. Cognitive coaching helps learners teach themselves through providing models and motivation for good learning.

9 **Reviewing and assessing learning:** *What have we learnt?*
Learners need time to review what they have done, to assess what they have learnt, and to draw out lessons or targets for the future. They need to learn how to assess their own learning. Positive feedback and feedforward make for future success.

10 **Creating powerful learning environments:** *What will help our learning?*
Children need support for learning, from their environment at school, at home, and in the community. What are the characteristics of powerful environments for teaching and learning? How do you create a learning community?

Included in each chapter are a number of tasks. These offer ways to explore the themes through teaching and learning activities with children. References and suggestions for further reading are given at the end of the book.

Teaching Children to Learn is not a recipe book that supplies easy answers. It seeks to offer a framework for a policy of active learning for any community, classroom or school. The process of improving teaching and learning, of developing the curriculum and assessing children's progress is a process of enquiry and research. If helping students to become more effective thinkers and learners is a valid goal of education, then this is a research project that involves us all.

Robert Fisher

1 Thinking to learn

How a thinking curriculum helps develop intelligence and learning

The basic ideas that lie at the heart of all disciplines are as simple as they are powerful. It is only when such ideas are put in formalised terms ... that they are out of reach of the young child.
  Jerome Bruner[1]

Isn't all education about helping us to think? Isn't that what we have a brain for?
  Sandip, aged 10

Young children are powerful learners. They begin communicating with their mothers from birth – using their body language in a dance of gestures and smiles. Some researchers suggest that this communicating and learning process begins even earlier, in the womb. Pregnant mothers, aiming to maximise the learning potential of their child, can begin by talking, reading, singing and playing favourite music to their unborn baby. Many who do so report feeling unexpected responses!

From an early age, the thinking child learns to master the most demanding of learning tasks, the acquisition of language. Children bring with them into the world an amazing strength of curiosity, an elasticity of thought, and an ability to ask and respond to deep and challenging questions, like these from 4 year olds: 'Why do people die?', 'What holds up the sky?', 'How does an oak tree fit inside an acorn?' This early curiosity often withers, through the effects of ageing and schooling. As one child said, 'I like school. You don't have to think. They tell you what to do.' Keeping a child's early questioning spirit alive can be one of the keys to success in learning. So how do you do it? How do you encourage a thinking child?

One way is to introduce the child to complex and abstract ideas. This can begin at an early age. A surgeon who was also a caring father was keen to develop the learning skills of his young son. The doctor specialised in brain surgery so he decided to share his enthusiasm and knowledge with his 3-year-old. First, he named parts of the brain, pointing to his head, and drawing large simple coloured pictures. Soon the young boy could identify the cerebellum and the cortex, and was saying to visitors in a quizzical way: 'How's your head?' By the age of 4, he had a better knowledge of parts of the brain than most adults, simply because the topic had been presented to him in a sophisticated but simple way by an enthusiastic adult.

All children are born with potential, and we cannot be sure of the learning limits of any child. But many children, including the very able and the 'strugglers', fail to fulfil their potential. The possible causes of educational failure and frustration are varied and often difficult to diagnose. Many however stem from what could be called 'cognitive confusion'.

Children suffer cognitive confusion when confronted with messages and demands that seem to make no sense. They are told to make a journey but they have no map. Children become confused and fail because of two broad factors:

- they cannot overcome blocks to learning
- they have not learnt how to learn.

Children need help to achieve their potential and to overcome the blocks to learning – the 'I don't know what to do', 'I can't do it', and 'I don't want to do it' responses – and to identify ways in which they can become effective learners – the 'I know what to do', 'I can do it (or at least try to do it)' and 'I want to try' attitudes. One way to begin thinking about learning is to try to identify what some of the blocks to learning might be.

TASK I

Identifying blocks to learning

What are some of the factors that can block learning?

1 Think about your own learning and consider the blocks you have experienced. It may be helpful to consider blocks to learning under three headings:
    - Factors within yourself – why did you find it hard?
    - Factors within the learning environment – what did not help you?
    - Factors within the subject matter of the learning – why was that hard to learn?
2 Discuss with children what they find hard to learn, and why they find it hard. Can they identify any of the blocks to their learning?

An 11 year old, encouraged to think about what the blocks to his learning were, identified the following list of factors:

- *in himself* – boredom, hunger, sickness, dyslexia (when your brain doesn't work as fast as other people's), tiredness, no interest
- *in the environment* – flies buzzing, ink running out, the person next to me disturbing (smashing my face in), no pen, no paper, no knowledge, no life
- *in the subject* – work is too hard, work is too long, work is illegible, no work to do, no subject (nothing to work about), work 'uninterests' me.

All children are 'at potential' in their learning, with the capability of exploring many paths of experience, and of creating new paths to explore – as in the lines of Robert Frost:

> *Two roads diverged in a wood, and I –*
> *I took the one less travelled by,*
> *And that has made all the difference*
>   from Robert Frost, 'The Road Not Taken'

All children, whatever their ability, are also 'at risk' – of being bogged down in lower forms of thinking and of endlessly repetitive experience, of not seeing new paths, of not knowing how to travel thoughtfully, of missing opportunities to explore fresh avenues of knowledge and experience. A good deal of research has gone into looking at the differences between successful and less successful learners. What does this research suggest are the best ways of helping a child think and learn more effectively?

Approaches to teaching thinking and learning skills

Traditionally there have been two approaches to teaching thinking and learning skills. One of these is to teach thinking through specific subjects or programmes. The other approach is to teach thinking and learning skills through all areas of the curriculum. Let us look at these two approaches in more detail.[2]

A specific programme . . . ?

In the past, specific subjects have been identified as those that will develop the ability to learn. Latin was once said to be such a subject, but research in the 1920s by Thorndike found that pupils studying Latin showed no measurable cognitive advantages over similar sets of students not studying Latin. There was no transfer from the rigours of learning Latin grammar into higher levels of thinking in other subjects. Pupils who learned Latin became good at Latin, and knowledgeable about grammar, Roman history and the roots of several European languages, but they did not become better thinkers and learners in any general sense.

Mathematicians have claimed that maths is the true foundation for logic and good reasoning, but there is no evidence that mathematicians are better thinkers and learners than others in any general sense. Maths reflects an important aspect of intelligence, but not all the modes needed for effective thinking. The same may be said for teaching the formal rules of logic. But what of science, is that not the queen of subjects, as it includes maths, logic and all forms of thinking about the real world?

Scientific method underpins much of modern progress, and recent research into science education suggests that children's general cognitive development can be enhanced though a particular approach to science education. This research is called the Cognitive Acceleration through Science Education project (CASE).[3] It aims to help both primary and secondary pupils to draw out certain key scientific principles, such as fair testing, probability and classification, by focusing on these in the discussion of scientific experiments. This drawing out of the principles that underlie scientific reasoning, the key concepts of rational investigation, helps students to transfer these principles into other areas of learning. Research shows that general levels of success can be raised through specific programmes aimed at developing children's thinking and learning skills.

Examples of specific programmes aimed at teaching thinking include:

- creative thinking courses, such as those of Edward de Bono
- Philosophy for Children programmes inspired by Matthew Lipman
- Instrumental Enrichment (IE) programmes created by Reuven Feuerstein.

Over 200 such programmes have been developed (mainly in America). But the big question remains: do the skills they aim to develop improve the student's ability to think and learn? The evidence does show that teachers who are enthusiastic and well trained in a programme produce good results. Teachers who are less keen and less certain about the value of what they are doing produce variable results. The message from research seems to be that programmes focusing on developing thinking skills can work and, in the hands of good teachers, do work. They show that you can teach children to think and reason more effectively and bring greater success in learning.[4]

. . . or thinking across the curriculum?

Another approach is to infuse the teaching of thinking skills into all aspects of the curriculum. This is achieved through involving children in active learning situations that extend their higher order thinking processes. In developing thinking across the curriculum, two of the questions that need to be asked are:

- What are the higher forms of thinking that students should be engaged in?
- What learning activities or approaches will develop higher order thinking?

According to research by Bloom,[5] lower levels of thinking involve knowledge (knowing the facts), comprehension (understanding the facts) and application (applying the facts). Higher levels involve analysis (taking the facts apart), synthesis (creating something new from the facts), and finally evaluation (evaluating the knowledge). These levels are said to represent the growing complexity and challenge to a child's thinking about any particular topic. (For more on Bloom's taxonomy, see page 20.)

The learning child is a thinking child. Successful learning involves helping children to move on to higher levels of thinking. These higher levels are characterised by what has been called 'metacognitive control'. Thinking can be seen as an information-processing capacity that involves input, output and control. It is through the exercise of metacognitive control that higher levels of thinking and learning can be developed (see Figure 1.1).

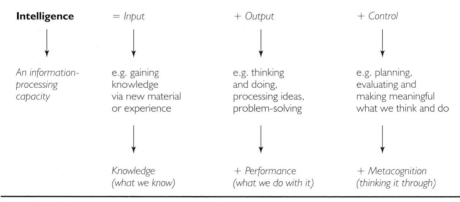

Figure 1.1 Intelligence as an information-processing capacity

Information can be processed in superficial ways so that it is easily forgotten. As Jamie, aged eight, said after a day at school, 'The words went in one ear and out the other.' Input, in the form of words, pictures or physical demonstrations is not enough to ensure learning. Output, in the form of activity related to learning, such as reading, writing or solving problems, helps the process of embedding learning in the memory. But activity alone is not sufficient for real learning because, when doing things, we do not necessarily think about them. Doing things is useful when practising mechanical skills ('Repeat after me . . .'). But doing things does not necessarily result in thinking or learning, as this snatch of classroom conversation illustrates:

Child: I have finished, Miss.
Teacher: Yes, but what have you learnt?
Child: Nothing Miss. You just asked me to do it.

Only by engaging higher order thinking, the executive or control areas of the brain, can we ensure that learning will be meaningful and will last. Thinking to learn involves challenging the learner to make sense of whatever the input and activity was – to ask not just 'What do you think?', but such questions as 'What did you learn?', 'How did you plan it?', 'How did you do it?', 'What did you find hard?' and 'What do you need to remember next time?' In responding to such questions, the sorts of questions good teachers ask and good learners ask themselves, we are not just processing bits of information but thinking about and learning how to learn.

Task 2 illustrates one aspect of our information-processing capacity:

TASK 2

Processing information

1 Look for about 10 seconds at this line of numbers, cover them and see how many you can remember by writing them down:
    1 0 1 0 0 1 0 0 1 1 0 1 0 0 1
2 How successful were you at remembering (processing the information)?
3 What strategy did you use to try to remember the information?
4 What helps us to remember and learn things by processing information?
5 Try this task with children. Discuss what helps them to remember.

Would practice on similar tasks improve their ability to process this kind of information? Try practising other memory games using words, pictures and objects.[6] Remember that it is the discussion of strategies that stimulates the thinking about learning. Just doing it is not enough.

Think about the ways in which the mind can try to process such information into the memory. The mind tends to remember more when it can link units of meaning into patterns. A famous psychological study showed that the human mind can recall about seven (plus or minus two) unrelated items of knowledge.[7] Memory can of course be trained, for example by making patterns out of the information given, and repeating these patterns until they become internalised as long-term memories. These patterns can created in visual ways, for example through remembering how things looked, verbally through how things sound, or physically through doing things such as writing things down to remember them. These patterns can be processed in different ways by the human brain. In what ways do you prefer to process information:

- *verbally* – through listening and saying or repeating the information
- *visually* – through seeing visual patterns, or pictures 'in the mind's eye'
- *logically* – through seeing a pattern of logical or mathematical relations
- *physically* – through physical representation or bodily gesture
- *musically* – through melody, rhythm or musical association
- *personally* – through linking information to personal experiences or memories
- *socially* – through learning with and from others, sharing a task?

There is not one way of remembering or learning, but many ways. Some people call different ways of learning *learning styles* (for more on learning styles, see page 14), others say they reflect different types of intelligence.

Multiple intelligences

Humans are unique in their ability to process information through these different facets of their intelligence. And human learning is most effective when it brings all its different capacities into play. The psychologist Howard Gardner argues that people have different ways of learning about the world and each of these reflects a different aspect or type of intelligence.[8] These multiple intelligences can be described in the following ways.

Linguistic or verbal intelligence

We know from brain studies that specific areas of the brain are responsible for different aspects of language use. The link between language and thought has been the focus of much research and debate. Does thought precede language, as Piaget taught, or is language the vehicle for thought, as Vygotsky argued? Thinking involves the use of words and concepts, and cognitive development is closely linked to conceptual development. One way of helping children to develop their thinking is to help them to pattern or map out their concepts and ideas. Concept mapping (see page 64) is one of a number of strategies that can help to enhance children's learning.

There are a various other ways in which the child's linguistic experience can be enriched, for example by:

- reporting and explaining their news and views
- giving instructions on how to do things
- verbal argument
- doing or creating crosswords and word games
- letter writing
- information finding – from newspapers, brochures, books, etc.
- reading and writing poetry
- writing their own journals.

Creating their own journal or magazine can involve many aspects of language experience. Groups of children can contribute to one 'publication', or produce their own personal publications. At the age of 10, T.S. Eliot created a magazine called *Fireside*. In a three-day period during the Christmas holidays he produced eight issues. Each one included poems, adventure stories, news, gossip and humour. In his childhood efforts lay the seeds of future genius.

Why not try to create your own journal or magazine?

TASK 3

Create a magazine

This can be a task for a child, or child and adult, or adults.

1　Create your own magazine or journal.
2　Identify a purpose and audience for your publication.
3　Plan what it could include.
4　Think of a title, and how it will be put together.

Questions beginning, Who . . . ? What . . . ? Why . . . ? When . . . ? Where . . . ? How . . . ? may help with planning. Use your linguistic intelligence – get publishing!

Visual/spatial intelligence

Evidence from brain research shows the left hemisphere dominant in processing language, with the right hemisphere crucial to visual and spatial processing. Visual spatial intelligence is needed for all forms of problem-solving that require visualising objects and patterns. The making and understanding of maps is an example of the use of visual thinking. Activities that can help develop visual thinking include:

- map-reading and navigating journeys
- creating maps, for example, of the neighbourhood or of imaginary worlds
- planning gardens, parks and recreation areas
- using diagrams and plans, for example in making models and construction toys
- designing routes or model layouts
- making a visual map of any given information, for example a recipe or story.

Goethe once said that we should talk less and draw more. Picasso completed 170 notebooks of sketches and experimental ideas, which he regarded as essential raw material for his finished work. Drawing involves many thinking skills, as does the critical appraisal of works of art and design. Other forms of spatial problem solving include visualising objects 'in the mind's eye' (can you see them from different angles?), and playing visual strategy games like draughts, chess and Othello. Some people are visual learners ('visiles') and learn best through visual means, but all of us can develop our capacity for close observation and visual thinking.[9]

TASK 4
Draw from your 'mind's eye'!
1   Choose a picture that interests you (such as a magazine picture, photo or art print).
2   Study it carefully using your eyes and your mind.
3   Try to visualise the picture in your 'mind's eye'.
4   Then hide the picture and draw it from memory, trying to recall it as accurately as possible.
5   Compare your drawing with the original. How could it be improved?
6   How could you improve your visual thinking?

Logical-mathematical intelligence

Logical-mathematical intelligence is what is involved in scientific thinking. Along with language (verbal reasoning), it is what is usually measured by IQ tests. The development of this kind of intelligence has been carefully researched by Piaget and other psychologists. Brain research shows that some areas of the brain play a more prominent part in mathematical calculation than others. But the actual mechanism that accounts for some being brilliant at maths is not yet properly understood. We do know, however, the sorts of activities which will strengthen this kind of intelligence. These include:

- budgeting – keeping personal and family accounts
- planning journeys and outings

- practising mental maths, for example calculating amounts spent, change given
- calculating odds, chances and probabilities
- estimating quantities
- managing and planning time
- making timetables
- solving logical puzzles and problems.

One of the characteristics of logical-mathematical intelligence is the ability to see patterns and relations between things. The following task is an example of a way in which pattern making can be encouraged:

TASK 5

Find a number pattern

1 Choose 10 or 12 random numbers and write them down.
2 Study them and see what links you can find between any of the numbers.
3 What patterns can you make with them? (For example, by putting them in order, by making sums from them, sets from them – such as odds/evens, primes, etc.)
4 What different patterns can you find?

Physical intelligence

Control of movement is localised in the motor cortex of the brain with each hemisphere controlling movement on the opposite side of the body, for example for right-handers control is usually in the left hemisphere. Many activities require physical (or kinaesthetic) intelligence to solve problems, and achieve desired results. Carrying out a mime sequence or hitting a tennis ball may seem very different from solving a mathematical equation. Yet the abilities to express emotion (as in dance), play a game (as in sport) or make a model (as in craft, design and technology) all involve physical problem solving. This sort of 'hands on' experience, wanting to solve problems physically is, as in all intelligences, more strongly developed in some than in others. But physical co-ordination has its corollary in mental co-ordination, and all physical tasks can benefit from a mindful approach. Physical intelligence is about developing mental muscles as well as the physical.

The following are some activities that can help develop physical intelligence, and physical problem-solving capacities:

- developing knowledge and skill in a chosen sport
- craft activity such as carpentry, clothes making, model making
- mastery of a physical discipline, for example a dancing, martial art or gymnastic skill
- cookery, for example biscuit making or cake making and decorating
- 3D puzzles, for example jigsaws, Lego
- machine maintenance, for example assembling, cleaning and maintaining mechanical appliances, such as a computer, bicycle or sewing machine.

The following task requires the application of physical intelligence:

TASK 6

Play a role

1 Choose a topic that you are currently reading, researching or learning about.
2 Think how to act, mime or role play some aspect of your learning experience. For example, mime a character from a reading book, television programme, historical period or foreign place, or plan a sequence of actions that illustrates something you have learnt.

Musical intelligence

Musical skill is another form of intelligence common to everyone. Studies of human development suggest that all children have some 'raw' musical ability. This natural response to rhythm and melody may have its genesis in the rhythm of the mother's heartbeat, and in the child's early attempts to understand the melodic pitch of speech sounds. Certain parts of the brain play important roles in the perception and production of music, largely in the right hemisphere. This intelligence can be highly developed in certain individuals. When he was three, Yehudi Menuhin was smuggled in by his parents to hear orchestral concerts. The young boy was so entranced by the sound of the violin that he wanted one for his birthday – and a teacher. He got both, and by the time he was 10 he was an international performer.

All children can be helped to develop their musical intelligence, and we know that training in reading music can help development in other areas of learning such as reading and maths. The following activities can help stimulate musical intelligence:

- humming or singing a chosen sound to tunes
- making music using a chosen instrument
- repeating songs heard clapping or beating time to music
- recognising and identifying tunes
- moving in time to music
- selecting appropriate music, for example background music for a story or poem.

TASK 7

Singalong

1 Put to music some words that you are reading or learning (sing them as a song).
2 Try writing a poem or rap and set it to your own music, or chosen musical melody and accompaniment.

Interpersonal intelligence

Interpersonal, or social, intelligence is about social awareness – the ability to understand and relate to others. As one child put it, 'I can't stand them, but I can *understand* them'. Piaget noted that one of the factors that limited the intelligence of young children was their egocentricity, namely the belief that the world revolves around them and their perceptions. Gradually, the child begins to notice differences in others, in their moods, temperaments, motivations and intentions. Interpersonal intelligence develops from this basic capacity, and shows itself in the growth of social skills and with the ability to empathise with and learn from others.

Two key factors relate to the development of interpersonal intelligence in humans. One is the prolonged period of childhood, including close attachment to the mother. That the mother has a crucial role to play in influencing the educational progress of children has been borne out in many studies. A second factor is the importance for humans of social interaction. As Vygotsky remarked, 'We first learn with others what later we can do by ourselves.' All children benefit from opportunities of learning with others, in pairs and small groups, as well as by teaching others. Part of what they learn by working and playing with others is the interpersonal skills that make for success in life, including knowing how to co-operate with, learn from and lead others.

Opportunities to develop interpersonal skills include:

- listening to others, for example to narratives, stories, poems, information and argument
- speaking to others, for example as above
- teaching others, for example showing and telling
- helping others learn/solve problems
- caring for younger children or others who need help or attention
- co-operating in a team, discussing and contributing to a joint effort.

The following activity utilises aspects of interpersonal intelligence:

TASK 8

Make a presentation

1   Prepare a presentation to others which includes explaining about what you are learning, a hobby or favourite pastime.
2   Show a visual element to illustrate your explanation.
3   Encourage the participation of others, for example by inviting questions or including an activity.

Metacognitive (or intra-personal) intelligence

Metacognition (self-awareness) is about the ability to understand and relate to oneself. It is probably the most important aspect of human intelligence, for it is linked to the processing of all other forms of intelligence. It is the 'me' in cognition. It is the access we have to our own thoughts and emotions, to what we think and feel, and why we do things. At the heart of metacognition is self-awareness – summed up in the words carved over the Delphic oracle: 'know thyself'.

Part of developing self-awareness is coming to know and understand one's mental states. From an early age, children have some understanding of the mind. By the age of three, they can use the terms 'know', 'think' and 'guess' to refer to mental states. By four, they understand what 'remember' and 'forget' means. By five, they are beginning to distinguish appearance and reality, and can answer the question 'Is it real or not real?' After five, they develop metacognition, through understanding more about the mind and brain, the different elements of personality. They know more about what it is to understand something, what they believe and how beliefs can change. This growth of metacognitive knowledge is a key factor in the success of learning – in knowing how to plan, predict, remember and find out.

The following activities can help in developing metacognitive awareness:

- keeping a personal diary or journal
- planning how to use time
- predicting what you will be able to do well or have difficulty with
- discussing and understanding your feelings and moods
- recognising who you are like or unlike (see below)
- setting and achieving personal goals
- reviewing and evaluating what you have done.

The following task can encourage metacognitive reflection:

TASK 9

Thinkwrite – about me

Get some paper, or your own book, and pen/pencil.
1 Think about yourself, or an area of your learning, and write under the following
   headings:
   Who am I?
   What I am good at?
   What I am not good at?
   What I find interesting?
   What I want to achieve?
   You might want to show this to others, or keep it to yourself!
2 If this description was read to your friends, without naming you, would they
   recognise you?
3 Ask your children to try this exercise.

Naturalist intelligence

Naturalistic or scientific intelligence is our capacity to investigate the physical world
and enables us in a systematic way to find out more about it. It begins with an enjoyment of the outdoors and the way this prompts curiosity about the world around us.
This sense of the mystery of things is what Einstein called the source of all true art and
science. Or as Frances, aged 10, put it: 'Every thing is a mystery because we don't know
everything there is to know about any one thing.'

Naturalist intelligence expresses itself through the human need to discover more about
the way the world works – as Blake said 'to see the world in a grain of sand . . .' It
prompts curiosity and enquiry about the everyday things around us. It encourages us
to make links between new learning and the natural world. It accounts for that human
urge to research, observe, collect, record and classify things.

Questions to develop naturalist intelligence include:

- What can you see? (Take a closer look.)
- What is this like? (Make a detailed description.)
- How is it different from . . . ? (Compare and contrast.)
- How has it changed? (*Consider changes* over time.)
- Why has it changed? (Think of reasons.)

Philosophical intelligence

Philosophical intelligence is what Gardner calls 'existential intelligence'. It expresses itself in the ability to ask deep questions about human existence such as the meaning of life and why we die. It is our capacity to investigate the metaphysical world, the world of values and ideas. As Tom, aged 13, put it:[10]

> *There are so many questions in life. School can give you answers from books, but most of the hard questions like 'Should I steal?' or 'Should I tell a lie?' or 'Does God exist?' you have to work out for yourself.*

Philosophical intelligence relies not on things within the world but on our thoughts about the world, the universe and everything. When a child asks 'What does "love" mean?' the question is philosophical if it is about the idea or concept of love. As Aristotle said: 'Philosophy begins in wonder.' It begins when we stop to ask 'Why?'

Young children are natural philosophers, not in the sense of coming to know all the answers, but in the sense of asking the sorts of questions that have puzzled philosophers for centuries, like the five year old who asked: 'Where does time go when it is over?' or the child who asked: 'Where is Grandma now she is dead?'

Philosophical intelligence is what all the great philosophers and spiritual leaders of the past have used in working out solutions to human problems about how to live and what to believe. Science can tell us what things are, but we need philosophical intelligence to help us see what to believe and how to behave. There is now a well-researched teaching methodology for engaging children in philosophical discussion and enquiry. [11]

The concept of multiple intelligences is a contested one. There is little empirical evidence to support the theory but it draws on a wide range of anthropological and biological knowledge – it seems to fit how humans respond to the world. Gardner originally identified seven intelligences and has added further ones. There may be other forms of intelligence, such as spiritual intelligence. Intelligences can combine. Emotional intelligence includes the interpersonal (social awareness and relationships) and the metacognitive (self-awareness and self-management) aspects of intelligence.

Traditional schooling has favoured verbal-linguistic and logical-mathematical intelligence – this may disadvantage children with strengths in other areas of intelligence. Thinking approaches to learning need to be applied to all aspects of intelligence, including the visual, verbal, musical, physical, social and personal. Children should be helped to understand and to value their many kinds of intelligence.

What does research into learning tell us?

Research into learning is rather like the old story of the blind men and the elephant. Each feels one part of the animal and thinks it is the whole animal. The following represent some of the main research findings from the last 30 or 40 years:

Piaget

Piaget emphasised the view that thinking was an activity. We should allow children to have *thinking time*. This was highlighted for me when I was helping a group of children to build some model bridges. One girl sat in the corner doing nothing while the rest were busily engaged on drawing, talking and assembling their bridges. 'Come on,' I said, 'get busy.' The girl looked pained: 'Can't I have time to think?' she asked. I then realised that although she was sitting there she was also being active – thinking. The trouble with thinking is that you cannot see it, which is why teachers often look for evidence of 'busy-ness'. What Piaget said we should look for are signs of *cognitive conflict*. To encourage children to higher levels of thinking, we need to challenge their ideas, and expect to be challenged, and to share what Yeats called 'the fascination of what's difficult'.

Bruner

Bruner's research emphasised the role of the teacher. It was not enough simply to let children think, work and play on their own. They need someone to *scaffold* their learning, to lead them on to higher levels. One way of doing this is to help children to focus on the key concepts of what they are learning, and then revisit these concepts again and again. He likened this process to a spiral, coming back on itself, but at higher levels. The 'spiral curriculum' means that if you wish to teach a child algebra at 14, you do best to begin at seven.

Vygotsky

The Russian psychologist Vygotsky found that social interaction was the key to success in learning. We learn more in collaboration with others – parents, other children and adults – than we can by ourselves. He rejected the view that intelligence was fixed. We all have what he called a *zone of proximal development*, referring to our potential for learning given assistance by others. We never know for sure how far this boundary stretches. The role of the teacher is to try to realise this potential in students, and the main means of that is through the use of language. 'Words,' said Vygotsky, 'are the tools of thinking.'

Linguistic theorists

Research by linguistic theorists has emphasised the value of talk in the development of thinking. We need to give children the opportunity to articulate their ideas, through talk and writing. In a sense we do not know what we think until we see what we say. The act of creating and communicating meaning forces us to think and rethink what we want to say, just as many teachers find that to get to know a subject really well you need to teach it. Or as one child put it, 'I didn't know I was going to say that until I said it!'

Curriculum research

Curriculum researchers have explored the way children construct their own theories. Gone is the view that children are blank slates on which to write, or empty vessels to fill. From an early age they are trying to make sense of the world, and constructing their own theories about how it works and their own place in the scheme of things. Research in maths and in science shows that children draw their own conclusions and ideas from what they see and do. And sometimes their theories are strange and ill-founded. As a child I was convinced that if you took a bulb out of a light socket the electricity would come flooding out. The trouble with wrong ideas is that they are very difficult to give up when they are your own. Even now my fears return whenever I am about to change a light bulb! Misconceptions can, however, be a spur to better thinking, providing we have a chance to discuss them with others. Learning occurs when there is a change in what we think, and good teaching is about helping children to construct and to reconstruct their ideas.

Cognitive research

Cognitive research has focused attention on the complex nature of thinking. The mind has been likened to a community of intelligences. We have a 'multi-mind'. Researchers have found that we all have different thinking and learning styles. Some of us are 'audiles', who prefer to hear the information, some are 'visiles' who prefer to see their information presented in visual form, and others are 'tactiles' who prefer concrete hands-on experience. Some prefer to work with others, with a partner or small group, and some prefer to work alone. The implication of these findings is that no one teaching style suits all students. What we need is a variety of strategies that can activate different facets of a child's intelligence.

Psychologists

Psychological research has emphasised the key role of *self-esteem*, and our sense of mastery over what we think and do. We are better motivated when we think we are going to do well, when we are confident in our abilities, as in the old adage: 'Success comes in cans not can'ts'. We need to build a sense of 'can do' in our children. One way of doing this is by helping them to recognise their own achievements, increasing their awareness of themselves as learners. Another is to communicate to children your high, but realistic, expectations of what they can achieve (for more on self-esteem and mastery learning, see Chapter 9).

Philosophers

Philosophy begins in wonder. Children share with the great philosophers a natural sense of wonder about the world. If they have around them people who can share in this wonder they are lucky indeed. Through the use of reason they can translate their curiosity into ideas, theories and hypotheses about the way the world works. For the philosopher Karl Popper the prime characteristic of humans is that they are problem solvers. And of problems there is no end. Children will need to be problem seekers and problem solvers. For Popper, the form of human organisation best fitted to solve problems is the 'open society' – a community of enquiry in which all can share (see page 54). The old schools of philosophy in Greece were places in which any topic or problem could be discussed, a useful model to offer the children we teach.

TASK 10

My theories of learning

Our ideas about learning come partly from our experience as learners and teachers, and partly from the example and ideas of others.

1 What has influenced you, and your ideas about learning?
2 Try to summarise your ideas about learning (in about 500 words), indicating what has influenced those ideas.
3 What are your theories about learning? Where do they come from?

Summary

The thinking child is a learning child. From an early age, able children can be introduced to complex ways of thinking, provided they are presented in simple and imaginative ways. Children are both 'at potential' and 'at risk' in their learning. If children are to realise their potential and avoid cognitive confusion they need to develop thinking and learning skills. Every lesson should be a lesson in thinking. One way of helping them is to focus on an aspect of thinking or intelligence in every lesson. Teachers need to offer a specific help in thinking and to infuse thinking across the curriculum. Research shows that we process information in different ways. Different ways to learn and different aspects of intelligence can be developed through a thinking curriculum. Children need to be taught to think for themselves.

2 Questioning to learn

How questions can help develop thinking and learning

He that questioneth much shall learn much, and content much; but especially if he apply his questions to the skill of the person whom he asketh; for he shall give them occasion to please themselves in speaking and himself shall continually gather knowledge.
Sir Francis Bacon (1561–1626)

It's harder asking questions than giving answers.
Jodi, aged 7

When someone asked Isidor Rabi, a Nobel prize-winning nuclear physicist, how he became a physicist he told the story of his mother who, when he came home from school, did not ask the usual question: 'So what did you learn today?' Instead she asked, 'Izzy, did you ask a good question today?'

It is at home that a child first learns the power of asking questions. One research study found that 4 year olds on average took part in 27 conversations per hour with their mothers, with each conversation averaging 16 turns.[1] Half of these conversations were initiated by the children, who asked about 26 questions per hour. There was little distinction between working-class and middle-class families noted in the amount, frequency or content of talk. The researchers reported 'passages of intellectual search', episodes of persistant enquiry through conversation, in all types of family. At home, children are usually 'partners in dialogue' with their parents. What then happens to children when they go to school?

The study showed that, when these children entered school, their conversations fell to 10 per hour with teachers, each lasting about eight turns, with teachers initiating most conversations and asking most questions. This and other studies show that apart from speaking less at school than at home, children were getting fewer turns, asking fewer questions, making fewer requests for information, using less elaborated sentences, expressing a narrower range of meanings and using language less often to plan, reflect, discuss or recall past events. There were fewer 'passages of intellectual search'. They are talked at rather than they are talked with. Such a discontinuity between the culture of home and school can lead to educational 'disadvantage'.

All learning is a form of enquiry. It is through asking questions that we find out about the world. The ways in which teachers, parents and care givers use language, and in particular use questions, can have immediate and long-term effects on children's learning. The purpose of this chapter is to look at ways of using questions to develop enquiring classrooms and enquiring minds.

Purposes of questioning

Why do teachers ask questions? The common response is that teachers use questions in order to motivate, to test knowledge and to promote reflection, analysis or enquiry. Questions are supposed to offer intellectual challenge, to encourage children to think. That is the theory. In practice, many of the questions teachers use inhibit intellectual activity, and save pupils from the effort of having to think. Research, such as the Leeds Project,[2] shows that most questions teachers use are closed, factual questions with known right answers, making low levels of cognitive demand that do not encourage children to persist in their thinking and learning. An example of this occurred in a classroom when a teacher asked a 6-year-old girl drawing a picture of a daffodil: 'What is this flower called?' The answer she received was: 'I think it's called Betty.'

Questioning can help facilitate learning. Through questioning a teacher can:

- focus attention
- arouse interest
- stimulate thinking
- find out what pupils know
- review, revise or recall learning
- invite everyone to engage in discussion
- engage individuals such as bright or shyer pupils
- probe children's understanding
- diagnose difficulties and misunderstandings
- stimulate curiosity and invite children's questions
- get pupils to explain, predict or give reasons
- help pupils express what they think, believe or know
- help pupils make leaning explicit
- help pupils apply their learning.

Questions can be used to stimulate higher order or lower level thinking (Figure 2.1).

Teachers ask a lot of questions. Perhaps they ask too many questions. Researchers found that a group of teachers asked on average more than 300 questions a day. The Oxford Pre-School Research Group,[3] who worked with nursery teachers and playgroup leaders, found that adults who asked more questions were:

- less likely to receive questions from children
- less likely to promote elaborated answers from children
- less likely to encourage children to contribute spontaneously to dialogue.

The more the children were questioned, the less initiative they showed in their responses. Most of the questions recorded in this study were of the closed variety. For example: 'What colour is it?', 'What is it called?', 'Where is it from?' Perhaps one of the lessons from this research is that we should try to ask fewer and better questions.

LIVERPOOL JOHN MOORES UNIVERSIT

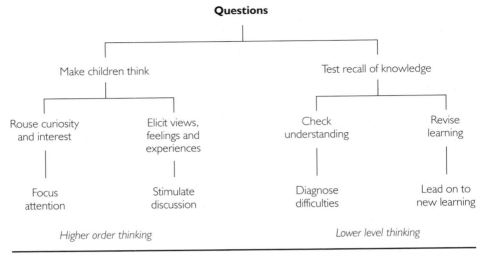

Figure 2.1 Some functions of questions

Asking the right question has been called the essence of teaching in the sense that it can provide a bridge between teaching and learning. Research into what makes schools effective places for learning identifies one common characteristic to be 'intellectually challenging teaching'.[4] One definition of a good question is that it provides an intellectual challenge. It stimulates what Piaget called the *cognitive conflict*, which may help children move on to a more advanced stage in their development. A good question can provide what Bruner calls the *scaffolding* to new learning. A good question is like a candle in the dark, shedding light on both truth and mystery. But not all questions facilitate learning. What differentiates a good question from an unproductive one?

Unproductive questions

A poor question is a dead thing, it leaves thinking where it was. Poor questions may limit, diminish or dismiss thinking. The following are some types of unproductive questions.

Stupid questions

These are questions that are thoughtless. They trivialise what is emotionally and intellectually complex. For example, a child whose mother had recently died was asked; 'How do you feel?' A stupid question will often provoke a thoughtless response. When the novelist T.H. White was asked by a doorstep evangelist whether he knew Jehovah, he replied 'I am Jehovah!'

Too complex questions

These are questions too big or too abstract to be tackled at once. Once, hurrying along a busy street, I was accosted by a man with a clipboard who asked: 'Do you believe in God?' Somewhat taken aback I replied. 'It depends what you mean by God.' As I moved on he said, 'I'll put you down as "don't know".' A teacher began a lesson with the question, 'Why is there pollution?' There was no response from the class. It may have been more productive to have narrowed the focus, to have created a context, and to have moved from the known to the unknown.

Too closed, narrow questions

These are often the 'what-is-the-teacher-thinking?' type of question. When too easy, they can result in the phenomenon of the hit-and-run barrage – 'What is this . . . ?', 'What is that . . . ?', 'What is the other . . . ?' When too hard, they can result in the teacher-answered question. A teacher once asked her class, 'What is a frog?' Getting no answer, she progressively answered the question herself - 'An . . . a . . . am . . . amph . . . amphib . . . amphibian!'

A major obstacle to thinking is the search for the 'quick-fix' of a single correct answer, the game of 'guessing what is in the teacher's mind'. The following example of this is taken from the Leeds Project research:

Teacher:	What day was it yesterday?
Child 1:	Tuesday
Teacher:	Was it?
Child 2:	Thursday
Teacher:	What day is it today?
Child 2:	Wednesday
Teacher:	Today is . . . What day is today?
Child 1:	Wednesday
Teacher:	What have we just had this morning? (No response.) What did we have this morning when we came to school?
Pupils:	Wednesday! Thursday!

There is a place for the quick, closed, fact-finding question of the quiz-type. A memory test can reinforce and remind pupils what they know, and can help them to remember. We all enjoy showing off what we know – when we know the right answer. For specific purposes, like mental arithmetic, low-level closed questions can provide a significant cognitive challenge. The acid test of a question is: does it provide a worthwhile challenge? In providing challenge, there needs to be a balance between the closed 'quick-fix' questions, and open questions that demand more complex and higher order thinking.

Higher and lower order thinking

Questions are broadly of three kinds:

- *empirical* – concerning facts about the world
- *conceptual* – concerning ideas, definitions and concepts
- *value-related* – concerning beliefs about the worth and merit of things.

These broad categories often overlap and sometimes a question can relate to all three types, for example 'What is a friend?' can be answered empirically by giving concrete examples from one's experience of the world, or conceptually by defining in a more abstract way the meaning of the word, or value-related by making a judgement about what a friend should be and do. Questions that are conceptual or value-related are often called *higher order* questions for they involve thinking at higher levels of abstraction.

Higher order thinking involves imposing meaning, finding structure in apparent disorder.[5]

According to Bloom's taxonomy of cognitive goals,[6] *analysis*, *synthesis* and *evaluation* demand more complex and 'higher' levels of thinking. Questions which ask for *knowledge*, *comprehension* and *application* demand less complex and thus 'lower' levels of thinking.

These aspects of thinking are reflected in the skills identified in the National Curriculum for England (1999). They can be characterised by certain key questions that can be asked during any learning conversation. Table 2.1 shows links between thinking skills, cognitive goals and these key questions.

Table 2.1 The links between thinking skills, cognitive goals and key questions

Thinking skills (National Curriculum)	Cognitive goals (Bloom)	Key questions
Information processing	Knowledge Comprehension Application	Who? What? Where? When? How? What do we mean by . . . ? What for? What other examples?
Reasoning	Analysis	Why? What is the evidence?
Enquiry		What more is there to find out?
Creative thinking	Synthesis	How can we add to or improve?
Evaluation	Evaluation	How do we judge or assess . . . ?

One effective questioning strategy is to ask questions which make increasing cognitive demands on students, to move from simple knowledge/recall questions, through questions that ask for comprehension/explanation and application, then analysis, synthesis and evaluation. Often this will mean moving from the 'Who', 'What' and 'How' descriptive question, to the 'Why', 'What for?' and 'What more?' question that asks for a more complex response. It is Socratic in the sense of moving from literal questions ('What is it?') through higher levels of abstraction ('Why?', 'How?') to conceptual questions ('What is the idea behind it?', 'What criteria do we use to judge it?'). A good question therefore fits into a pattern that offers progressive and productive challenge to learning. It offers a model for the sorts of productive question that students can ask of themselves and of others.

Good questions

Research shows that many teachers fall into the trap of asking too many questions – too many closed and low-level questions. We get a better learning response from children if we try to:

- *Ask fewer but better questions.* A few questions we really need to think about are better than 10 that we do not need to think much about. Aim for quality rather than quantity of questions.
- *Seek better answers.* With fewer questions, we have time to invite more responses, and to extend thinking time. Withhold the rush to judgement; work at getting a better response.
- *Encourage children to ask their own questions.* The ability to question is one of the keys to effective learning, and it comes with practice. Value children's questions as much as their answers.

One of the characteristics of a good question is that it avoids the trap of a 'yes' or 'no' response. When one teacher was getting her children to evaluate their work, she asked, 'Are you pleased with the way it's worked out?' As she listened later to a tape of the discussion, she realised her question required only a yes/no response. 'How well do you think it has turned out?' would have invited more.

Examples of open-ended questions, which genuinely invite children to think, include:

What do you think . . . ?
How do you know . . . ?
Why do you think that . . . ?
Do you have a reason . . . ?
How can you be sure . . . ?
Is this always so . . . ?
Is there another way/reason/idea . . . ?
What if . . . ?/What if not . . . ?
Where is there another example of this . . . ?
What do you think happens next . . . ?'

A good question makes the mind buzz, it offers a challenge to thinking, a search for understanding. They are troublesome, rarely rooted in certainty and invite an open-ended, thoughtful response. They are productive for they generate something new. Examples of such questions could include:

- *Judging* – Is it ever right to steal/tell a lie/kill someone?
- *Comparing* – In what ways are these two objects/pictures/texts/actions similar? In what ways are they different?
- *Evaluating* – Which is the better picture/text/object/action . . . ? Why?

The best questions provide both challenge and interest. Consider the topic of butterflies. What questions might arouse a student's interest? How might you challenge his/her thinking about butterflies? How would you use questions to engage higher levels of thinking? Consider some alternatives, for example:

- *Concrete/literal questions* – What is a butterfly? What do you know about butterflies?
- *Analytic/creative questions* – How is a butterfly different from a bird? Would you rather be a butterfly or a bird? Why?
- *Abstract/conceptual questions* – What species is a butterfly? What defines an insect?

TASK 11

Plan a Socratic sequence of questions

Choose a topic you are planning to teach. Plan a sequence of questions about the topic, suitable for your chosen audience.

- Devise concrete or literal questions to begin your sequence.
- Move on to questions which require analysis and lead on to an abstract or organising concepts.

Remember that the best questions cannot always be planned. As one teacher reports: 'My best questions come from listening to a child's response to an initial question and asking for more information, detail or explanation.' Sometimes the best questions come from the children themselves. Begin, for example, with the open question: 'What would you like to know or ask about this?' Use a prompt or stimulus, such as a picture (for example, a concept cartoon in science) or physical demonstration. Ask them to choose what they think are the best questions. Discuss which are the best questions, and why.

A teacher of a class of 13 year olds was due to give a lesson in science on gravity. She thought a useful way to start would be to find out what the pupils already knew about the concept. So to begin the lesson she wrote on the board the following questions:

- You drop a ball from your hand. It falls. Why?
- You are standing on the surface of the moon. You drop a ball. What happens? Why?

The class were divided into small groups to discuss their ideas about each of the questions, and to record their conclusions. The questions stimulated a variety of explanations, many expressing assumptions in unscientific terms. In response to the first question, one group stated: 'The ball falls because of the air.' Answers that mentioned the key word, 'gravity', provided no insight into the level of real understanding. In response to the second question, another group wrote: 'The ball drops very slowly because the gravity on the moon is much less than on earth.'

The collection of this information took 20 minutes, and the pupils enjoyed the exercise. It was the first time the teacher had used such a questioning strategy, and later commented she 'was amazed by the range of ideas that the pupils came up with'. The act of writing down responses to the questions is a way of making explicit the students' initial ideas and provides a reference point against which any development of ideas can be judged. And when we are given answers to our questions – whether in written or verbal form – how should we respond?

Thinking time

'What is truth?' said jesting Pilate and would not stay for an answer. When you have asked a question, how long do you wait for an answer? A good answer is worth waiting for. The composer Stravinsky once advised musicians: 'Value your intervals like dollars.' And in questioning we should learn to value silence.

Research has shown that some teachers on average wait only one second for an answer. If an answer is not forthcoming within a second, teachers tend to interject by repeating or rephrasing the question, asking another question or another child. When a pupil answers, teachers tend to respond within one second, either with praise, or by asking another question or with a comment. Rarely, it seems, are students allowed the luxury of a thoughtful silence. We want to keep the conversational ball rolling, but studies show that by increasing thinking time, also called 'wait time,' the quality of pupil's responses can be dramatically increased.

How long should we allow for thinking time? Increasing 'wait time' to 3 seconds can result in significant changes, such as:

- pupils giving longer answers
- more pupils offering to answer
- pupils willing to ask more questions
- pupils' responses becoming more thoughtful and creative.

Strangely, teachers find it very difficult to sustain a longer waiting time. Old habits die hard and the 'scattergun' approach of quick-fire questions and answers soon reappears. And it is not only pupils who need time to think. There are two elements to thinking time – after the question and after the answer:

- *thinking time 1* – allowing 3 seconds after the question to encourage longer, more thoughtful answers from pupils
- *thinking time 2* – after the answer, the teacher models a thinking response, values complexity and defers judgement.

Allowing silence is therefore a deliberate act by the teacher to encourage a more thoughtful response, as in this example:

Teacher: What makes a good piece of writing?
Child 1:   When you write neatly
Teacher: Hmm . . . (pauses)
Child 1:   Like it's a good story . . . and it's easy to read.
Teacher: Ahh . . . easy to read. What else?
Child 2:   Well, it has to have a good beginning or you don't want to carry on . . . I mean it's got to be exciting . . . make you want to go on reading it.

Questions that can help us focus on the ways we use talking for thinking include:

- Who is doing the talking and the thinking?
- Am I allowing enough thinking time? (Thinking time 1 and 2?)
- Do I support students in their talking and thinking? How?

There are various ways in which pupils can be helped to participate and to make their own meanings. What fuels their response? Different students need differing sorts of stimulus. Often the 'puzzled listener' role will be effective, if it reflects genuine interest and attention to the student's answer. Strategies to support thinking and talking include 'pause–prompt–praise':

- *Pause* – giving time, thinking time, and opportunities for rethinking and restating an idea – 'Can you explain/Tell us again . . . ?'
- *Prompt and probe* – giving verbal encouragement, for example by 'reflecting back' to check whether we have understood what the student has said. Following the pupil's train of thought and encouraging deeper exploration is sometimes called 'probing'. Examples of probing questions include:

- Why do you think that . . . ?
- How do you know . . . ?
- Can you tell me more about . . . ?
- Can you show me what you mean?
- What if . . . ?
- Is it possible that . . . ?

Sometimes a minimal encouragement will prompt further response – 'Hmmm', 'Umm', 'Uh huh', 'Yes . . . ?', 'OK . . .', 'I see . . .', 'And . . .'

Non-verbal reinforcement includes eye contact ('The eyes are the windows of the soul'), facial signals such as smiles, body gestures such as nodding (nodding on rather than nodding off!) and other signals of approval.

- *Praise* – giving positive feedback. Being specific and personal with praise – 'That's an interesting answer Jan', 'Thanks for that answer Pat' – can foster general participation by:
  - supporting the hesitant
  - rewarding the risk takers
  - valuing every genuine contribution.

One way of valuing and encouraging contributions is to put all ideas and suggestions on display, perhaps with the child's name next to each contribution, as a focus for further discussion, writing or research.

Questioning skills

The skilful use of questioning can help turn the classroom into a 'community of enquiry' in which all are involved (see page 54). Kerry[7] has identified seven questioning skills:

- pitching the language and content level appropriately for the class
- distributing questions around the class (to the shy as well as the 'stars')
- prompting and giving clues where necessary
- using pupils' responses (even incorrect ones) in a positive way
- timing questions and pauses between questions
- making progressively greater cognitive demands through sequences of higher-order questions
- using written questions effectively.

There is a danger, even with skilful questioning, of following a pre-set agenda, and not encouraging children to take some initiative in a discussion. In adopting a 'teacherly role', we can dominate the talk by asking too many questions and imposing our own meaning. Repeating a fixed pattern of questions – Who? What? Where? When? – will result in children giving short answers, not responding to each other, offering fewer ideas and asking fewer questions.

Alternatives to questions

Some alternative strategies can prove more effective in stimulating thoughtful discussion. One strategy is the Socratic method of 'scholarly ignorance', that is playing the puzzled listener, keeping the discussion open, inviting to say more, using 'pause–prompt–praise' and other alternatives to questions.

One way to avoid excessive teacher control is to actively encourage pupil-to-pupil exchanges. Some ways to do this include:

- *Withholding judgement* – respond in a non-evaluative fashion, ask others to respond.
- *Inviting alternative responses* – 'There is no one right answer.', 'What are the alternatives?', 'Who's got a different point of view?'
- *Inviting children's questions* – 'Would anyone like to ask a question?', 'Who has got a question?'
- *Inviting children to question each other* – 'Pat, will you ask someone else what they think/for their ideas?'
- *Using think–pair–share* – allow thinking time, discuss with a partner, then share with the group.

Teachers who ask too many questions tend to discourage students from giving elaborate or thoughtful answers. Those who force on pupils a pattern of repetitive questions – Who? What? Where? When? Why? – will face pupils who ask fewer questions themselves, give short responses, rarely discuss with peers, volunteer few ideas and show many confusions. What then is to be done? One answer is to use alternatives to questions.

Think alouds

Thinking is talking it through with yourself when you have a problem.
Laura, aged 10

Teachers (including parents and any care-givers) who model thoughtfulness will encourage their children to exhibit more thoughtful behaviour. Teachers who offer their own thoughts and ideas, who speculate, suggest and hypothesise, will create an environment in which speculation, hypothesis and argument can flourish. As a teacher I would regularly talk to myself, 'thinking aloud', and through this gained not only a useful reputation for eccentricity but also found my pupils more willing to think and talk things through for themselves.

The sorts of questions I would ask, as 'think alouds', to model self-regulation of the thinking process might include:

- What am I going to do/write/say now?
- What is my problem? What sort of problem is this? Where have I seen this before?
- What am I doing now? What do I need to do? What can I try?
- Who can help me? What do I need? What is the next step?
- How am I doing? How will I do it? How have I done?
- Is there a better way? What alternatives are there? What must I remember?

Talking it through

I learn more when I have time to talk it through.
Benny, aged 9

We use questions as a way of extending dialogue with children. Rather than accepting short answers, we support learning if more extended answers are sought. This can be encouraged if the teacher sometimes takes on a more challenging role, for example by agreeing or disagreeing, putting an opposing argument or not rewarding children for simply making a response. We want them to think more and to say more. If something is worth thinking and talking about, how do we extend the dialogue?

The following are kinds of 'talking it through' statements that can encourage more thoughtful and extended responses:

- *a speculative statement*, for example 'Perhaps . . .', playing 'devil's advocate' to stimulate response
- *a reflective statement*, for example 'You seem to be saying that . . .', to encourage elaboration
- *a state-of-mind statement*, for example 'I don't quite understand . . .', to invite further response
- *a request for information*, for example 'I'd like to hear what you think about . . .', to extend discussion
- *an invitation to think*, for example 'I want you to think carefully about this . . .', to cue a more thoughtful response, or to invite a question.

Children learn more when they have time to talk things through and have the time and confidence to ask their own questions. How do we encourage children to question?

Encouraging children to question

If we want pupils to be active and adventurous thinkers, we need to encourage them to ask questions. As children become older this becomes less easy. Researchers[8] found that those children who were asking over 50 per cent of questions at home, were asking under 5 per cent of the questions once they got into school. So how can we encourage pupils to be more active in questioning and seeking after knowledge? Two ways of trying to establish a climate of enquiry are for teachers to:

- model a questioning mind by thinking aloud and asking good questions
- value and provide opportunities for students to ask questions.

When a class of 10-year-olds were starting the study of a country, the children were put into groups to brainstorm questions on: *What do we want to know about our country?* The groups were then to share, display and discuss their questions which were to act as stimulus-points for the research project.

In a class of younger children, someone had brought in a snail. The teacher could have used the snail simply as an opportunity for 'look and say', but after the usual knowledge/understanding questions – 'Where was it found?', 'What do you know about snails?', 'Where can you find out about snails?' – she encouraged the children to ask their own questions. They soon came up with the usual sorts of questions – 'Can they hear?', 'What do they eat?', 'How do they move?', and the one they found most interesting, 'Do snails love each other?' There was a lively discussion about ways to find answers to this question!

If children themselves identify what they want to know, by asking a question, they are much more likely to value and remember the answer. Some questions will not be easy to answer. One teacher, when asking children if they had any questions about current news, was asked, 'What is the difference between the ozone layer and the greenhouse effect?' She did not feel able to give a full answer at the time, so she gathered a variety of responses from the children, displayed the question in the classroom, involved them in researching an answer and even got in an 'expert' to judge the different answers to the question.

This brings us to another characteristic of questions – like good wine, questions can improve with keeping. Display them, savour them, come back to them. Find some more. Sort them into categories, for example:

- questions we can answer
- questions we can find the answer for
- questions that cannot be answered.

Discuss with children the nature of questions. Give them a list of questions and ask which out of a list of questions they think is the best or most interesting. Discuss good and bad questions. Find out what questions they would like to have answered. Can they think of a question that can never be answered? Create a poem about questions (see Figure 2.2).

TASK 12

Generating questions

In this task, children generate and discuss questions on a chosen topic. The teacher also brainstorms/devises some back-up questions.

1 Ask children to generate questions on a chosen topic in twos or threes.
2 Share and analyse questions together. How many different questions were created?
3 Discuss the kinds of questions that were asked.
4 What were the most interesting questions? What made them interesting?

When asked how many questions might be asked about the topic in hand, one child responded, 'Endless'. When asked to explain he said, 'They are endless because we would never know what everyone in the world might think and say. There could always be another question.'

One way of encouraging children to ask questions is to have a Think Book or Learning Log in which children can write about what they feel and think, and be invited to answer that key question in all learning – 'What does this mean to me?'

> What is the mystery
>   of the funny
>   question mark?
>   How
>   does
>   it
>   happen?
>   Did
>   someone
>   twist
>   the
>   long
>   exclamation mark
>   so
>   it
>   had
>   a head?
> That's how they
> found out
> a new
> meaning
> to
> this thing.
>
>
> Do you
> under-
> stand?

Figure 2.2 Poem by Karen, aged 10: 'What is the mystery of the funny question mark . . . ?'[9]

Assessing the ability to question

A simple way to assess the ability of children to devise questions is to give them a common object such as a chair or cup and ask them to list as many questions about the object as they can. Another way is to take a subject of current study and see how many questions children can create about the topic. A third way is to choose a text, such as a part of a story or poem and see how good they are at interrogating the text by asking them to create questions about it. With practice at creating questions from a variety of source materials, the fluency and flexibility of their questioning will improve. After a year in an enquiring classroom, children will often be able to generate twice as many questions, under test conditions, as they were able to create at the beginning of the year.

Looking at an object – some questions that can be asked

Test your questioning power by choosing any everyday object and seeing how many questions you can create about that object. How many questions do you think it is possible to generate? (The answer is not known, for the possibilities are theoretically limitless.)

The following are some of the kinds of questions that children can create after looking at an object. Given practice in asking questions they will be able to see more, to think more and learn more about any object or aspect of life – and should with experience improve the quality and quantity of their questioning.

- *Physical features*
  What is it? What is it called?
  What does it look like? What colours/shapes/textures does it have?
  What does is it feel/smell/sound like?
  What is it made of? Is it made of natural or manufactured materials?
  Is it complete? Has it been altered, adapted or mended?
- *Construction*
  How was it made?
  Who made it?
  How was it made?
  Was it made by hand or machine?
- *Function*
  What was it made for?
  How has it been used?
- *Age*
  Is it old?
  How do you know?
- *Value*
  Is it valuable? Who is it valuable to? Why is it of value?
  What is it worth?
  What is 'value'?
- *Origin*
  Where does it come from?
  Where was it made?
- *Design*
  How is it decorated?
  Is it well designed? Why do you think that?
  How could it be improved?

Creating a questioning classroom

There can be problems in creating an enquiring classroom – a place where questioning is valued and encouraged. The questions of children can be challenging and unsettling. It will not suit the teacher who thinks they have all the answers. It will not suit the teacher who is afraid of being intellectually challenged. It will suit the teacher who is keen to help children to be independent, creative and curious. It will also help to keep alive their own curiosity about the world, and about themselves. In an enquiring classroom, I was once asked, 'Mr Fisher, what are you going to do when you grow up?' In another, I thought I would offer a philosophical challenge to some 9 year olds. I said, 'How do you know that I am Mr Fisher?' After a silence, one child replied thoughtfully, 'How do you know *you* are Mr Fisher?'

However these questions are answered, perhaps there is a clue to creating an enquiring classroom in the mnemonic – PARTS ARE EQUAL – reportedly used in the human awareness training of traffic wardens, meaning: 'People Always Respond to Someone Actively Encouraging Equality in Questioning and Listening.'

The following are some examples of classroom activities designed to create questions for thinking.

Question of the day

Display the question of the day for children to see at the start of the day. Use think–pair–share. Give children time to think about the question (or draft responses), discuss with a partner, then share and discuss as a whole group.

Study questions

Help pupils identify what is significant in their learning. Groups devise questions from their study, writing or textbook, to test themselves or others.

Reading review questions

Ask your pupils to help you to ask the class questions about the story they are reading or listening to. Try to get the children to identify what kind of question it is, for example is the question asking for information that is 'on the lines' (explicit), 'between the lines' (implicit) or 'beyond the lines' of the story?

Hotseating

A pupil chooses to be a character from literature, history or current affairs. The others brainstorm questions to ask the child in role. Encourage open questions.

Twenty questions

One or more pupils chooses either an object, person or place. The others have 20 questions to find out what it is. Only 'Yes' or 'No' answers are allowed and a limit of three direct guesses is allowed. Play in groups of six (two select the topic, four ask the questions).

Question and answer

The pupils devise questions to fit given answers, for example for younger children a person, place, thing or number; for older children a quote from a poem or play.

Any questions?

Students ask or write any question (real, hypothetical, factual or metaphysical). Each question is then given to an 'expert' partner to answer.

Interview questions

Decide on someone to interview, for example a visitor or a local VIP. Ask the pupils to devise, share, evaluate and prioritise the best interview questions.

Question your classroom

Devise, write and display questions to stimulate thinking and discussion about objects, pictures or texts of interest in your classroom.

Questions box, board or book

Collect any interesting or puzzling questions that arise in the classroom. Create a place to write, store or display your questions, such as in a box, on a board (or Wonder Wall) or in a special book. Set aside some time, such as at the end of the week, to choose and discuss a question. Alternatively share out the questions for children to work on at home or swap questions with another class or group.

ICT to develop questioning and dialogue

Use computers, including email and web site pages, to extend the opportunities for questioning, interaction and dialogue. Use the interactive whiteboard to allow children to engage with a focal question or to develop questions within a lesson.

TASK 13

Creating a questioning classroom

Consider the following questions. Compare your answers with those of colleagues. Discuss ways of developing a questioning classroom.
1　What is the value of children asking questions?
2　Who asks most questions in your classroom?
3　Is the importance of questioning discussed with children?
4　How can we encourage children to ask more questions and better questions?
5　Where is evidence of children's questions on display in the classroom or school?
6　What examples are there of children asking interesting and relevant questions?
7　How can we use ICT to develop questioning, interaction and dialogue?
8　How do you create an enquiring classroom?

Summary

Questioning lies at the heart of learning and teaching. Some teachers ask too many closed and unproductive questions. We should aim to ask fewer but better questions, and seek from our students better answers, giving them time to think and to respond. Teachers help children learn by being discriminating in their use of questions, and by encouraging students to ask their own questions. All children should have opportunities to generate questions and their ability to do so will improve with practice. We should aim to create enquiring classrooms – where children's questions are valued, and where genuine learning and understanding are promoted.[10]

3 Planning to learn

Learning to plan is an essential skill for learning how to learn.

The best generals are those who arrive at the results of planning without being tied to plans.
Winston Churchill (*My Early Life*)

I've got a plan, it's quite complicated and may not work, but at least it's a plan.
Leonie, aged 9

Learning to learn is about learning to think, and in particular about thinking ahead. Planning is about mentally rehearsing what we are going to do in a systematic way. Thinking ahead is a key to human success. Planning is a habit of intelligent behaviour. But children often do not realise the importance of thinking ahead and may not get systematic instruction in planning. They learn how to perform tasks and procedures, but are not taught the importance of planning. If planning is important then children need help in learning to plan. But are there general planning and problem-solving skills? If so, what are they and how do we teach them?

Experts and novices

One way to investigate whether there are general problem-solving skills is to look at the way expert problem solvers work. What factors make for successful performance in varying fields of human endeavour? When looking at expert performance in diverse fields, such as mathematics, athletics, art, novel writing, science or cookery, one common factor is that experts spend more time in planning and preparing for their activity than novices. Problem-solving in any area of human endeavour is complex and makes considerable demands on cognitive skill and processes of premeditation. Whether it is for cookery or calculus, some essentially similar mental habits are followed. Where outcomes are successful, there have been efforts to plan the process, to adapt and refine the operation of the activity, and to keep performance under review.

Experts have more knowledge than novices, but more importantly they have the habits and intelligent behaviour related to a particular domain. They spend more time in mental rehearsal, planning and preparation. They also have the skills and strategies that allow them to deal with problems and turn thoughts into successful action. Many of the problems that we, and experts, face each day have common elements.[1] Every problem-solving situation requires a decision (even a decision to make no decision), a plan of action, a set of actions, and a way in which to tell if our goal has been achieved. Are these skills of a general nature or are they particular to every situation?

There has been much debate about whether there are any general problem-solving skills that can be applied to a number of different tasks. One view is that problem-solving means having specific knowledge relevant to a particular situation. Many subject teachers in secondary schools subscribe to the view that the special skills and knowledge that they teach are subject specific and non-transferable. However, others argue that there are a number of general competencies that are involved in all problem-solving activities regardless of the subject or specific situation. These general skills relate in particular to planning, monitoring and evaluating, what has been called the cycle of 'plan–do–review'.[2]

Planning for problem solving

In some cases students will need specific instruction in what strategy to employ. At other times, awareness of more general problem-solving processes may be all that is needed to tackle a specific task. Typically, direct instruction is needed for novice learners and those with learning difficulties. For students who are older and have well established basic skills, more general problem-solving procedures may be more appropriate. These general problem-solving processes can be summed up in the following steps:

1 *Define the problem* – what do we want to achieve?
2 *Gather information* – what do we need to know to tackle the problem?
3 *Form a strategy* – how can we tackle the problem?
4 *Implement the strategy* – how are we tackling the problem?
5 *Monitor outcomes* – have we achieved our aim?

Successful problem solving involves the systematic application of a sequence of thoughts and activities – in other words, planning. A plan is a set of steps or sequences that we believe will lead to success in a task. A plan does not need to be a set order of steps. Often plans need to be flexible to allow for the use of a range of possible strategies that may help in achieving our objective. As we move to a solution, we may need to try out new ideas, to take account of new obstacles and changing circumstances. Planning in its simplest form means we have thought about what we are going to do. 'Chance favours the prepared mind,' said Pasteur. In teaching children how to plan, we are teaching them to be thoughtful about what they are doing, to be best prepared to achieve success in learning.

Some researchers regard planning as the most important of the cognitive methods that we can use in the classroom.[3] Planning helps students to deal with information in any subject in an organised and systematic way. Planning can be regarded as the key working process of the brain in its higher functions, and fundamental to the success of human learning.[4] Even very young children can begin to link actions together to achieve goals. Planning is evident in the way children solve construction problems with building blocks, persuade parents to let them watch an extra hour of TV or unfasten child-proof locks. Young children do not recognise that they are creating plans, and they could not explain the planning process to others. However, they do come to understand the distinction between mental activity (such as wanting things) and actions (such as eating food).[5] They are able to manipulate in their minds simple mental constructs and ideas of physical things to achieve certain goals. It is a functional understanding. They do not consciously recognise that certain actions are necessary to achieve a goal. It is only later that they come to understand what they are doing and why. They become aware of the concept of a plan, that certain actions can be linked together in a conscious and premeditated fashion to achieve certain goals. Plans begin to become 'blueprints for thinking'.[6]

Young children learn how to perform tasks before they are able to understand what they are doing and why. This development of understanding has implications for educators. Children need help in gaining insight into ways of performing tasks successfully. They need help in understanding and in making use of various levels of planning. These levels of planning can be summarised as:

- unconscious planning
- specific planning
- strategic planning.

Unconscious planning

In unconscious planning, the person performs the task without being aware of a plan, or the need for a plan. Problem solving is then a matter of doing rather than design. To the question 'Why are you doing that?' the child might reply, 'I don't know, I just do it and it comes right.' Certain kinaesthetic tasks, such as riding a bike or building a tower with blocks, may not require conscious planning. The danger is that some children apply this level of undifferentiated planning to all learning tasks, regarding success in problem solving as something to do with good fortune or coincidence rather than design − 'You either can do it or you can't.'

Specific planning

Specific planning involves a conscious effort to develop a plan for a specific task. The individual is aware of the goal and can articulate some steps in helping to achieve the goal. For example, a child makes a plan of a story before writing it, or an adult plans the layout of a new garden. There is a systematic attempt to reach a goal, but there may not be awareness of other strategies or approaches to the problem. In particular, a specific plan may founder on an unexpected obstacle. A problem arises and the plan does not seem to work. To the question, 'What will you do if you get stuck?' or 'What happens if it does not work?' there may not be an answer, if the planning is too narrowly specific.

Strategic planning

Strategic planning is deliberate planning activity that includes consideration of potential obstacles and the need for flexibility in the use of strategies. An approach to a task may include a number of alternative routes. Planning is flexible to include changes in the sequence as circumstances and conditions allow. Examples might include the tactics devised by a sports team to cope with varying conditions of play, or the way children might plan to create a magazine together to take account of different contributions in the group. To be effective, strategic planning needs a conditional element, reflected in the question 'What would happen if . . .' It recognises the need for alternative plans of action if events or circumstances change.

One planning framework that can be applied to any problem is the TASC model (Thinking Actively in a Social Context).[7] This approach stresses the social context of planning, that good planning is the result of social activity, in particular discussion and dialogue with others. It presents the stages of a problem-solving process that can act as a planning tool, first for the teacher and then the pupil. The stages need to be explicitly taught and modelled by the teacher so that they become internalised as a model for children to follow when faced with any problem or learning challenge.

The stages of the TASC model are:

1 *Gather and organise* – what do we already know?
2 *Identify* – what is the problem?
3 *Generate* – what ideas can we think of?
4 *Decide* – which is the best idea?
5 *Implement* – what do we do or make?
6 *Evaluate* – how well did we do? How can we do better?
7 *Communicate* – how can we share our ideas?
8 *Reflect* – what have we learned?

However, no matter what problem-solving steps or process we go through 'the best laid plans of mice and men oft gang astray'. Why? One reason is that the various elements of our planning process need to come under metacognitive control.

Planning and metacognition

Metacognitive control is one of the characteristics of good thinking and learning. Students with good metacognitive control (meta-students) are active in their responses, mindful, internally controlled, strategy aware and strategy efficient. Those with poor metacognitive control (non-meta-students) are passive, unreflective, impulsive, externally controlled, strategy unaware and strategy inefficient. They tend to have the episodic grasp of reality that characterises poor learners.

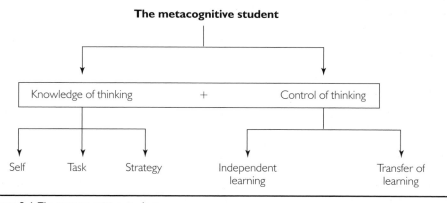

Figure 3.1 The metacognitive student

Metacognition has three major elements:
1 *Planning*
   • planning goals (and subgoals), operations and sequences
   • identifying obstacles and possible problems
   • knowing the process and predicting outcomes.

2 *Monitoring*
- keeping in mind the goals
- place in the sequence
- possible obstacles and errors
- knowing what to do when things go wrong or plans fail
- knowing when goal is achieved.

3 *Assessing*
- assessing success of strategies and progress towards goal achievement
- assessing errors and mistakes along the way
- evaluating the whole process.

The best way to encourage pupils to think about planning is to model the process yourself. It is becoming routine for teachers to demonstrate how writers plan their writing and designers plan their projects. However, evidence from research shows that whereas modelling the process (what we should do) is normal, modelling thinking (what we think as we plan it) is less common. Teachers should model their 'strategic thinking' and help children to talk through various possible ways of approaching a task or solving a problem. The planning of good readers and writers, mathematicians and scientists is largely unobservable, which is why teachers need to model it for their pupils in all lessons. Meta-planning is about becoming aware of choices or strategies, in whatever we are doing, becoming conscious of why choices are made so enabling learners to take control of their own thinking and learning.

The aim is to model the vocabulary we want children to use in their own planning by using it ourselves to describe our teaching, with such prompts as 'What do we need to think about first?', 'What are we trying to achieve?', 'What strategy could we use?' Such dialogic teaching helps develop metacognitive awareness when a teacher asks questions that probe the child's assumptions about their learning. It develops their awareness in planning of:

- *Self* – what must I remember?
- *Task* – what must I do?
- *Strategy* – what plans do I have?

and the capacity to question their own planning – 'Is this the best plan?'

Research tells us that the brain cannot think about a task and think about thinking (meta-think) at the same time. The brain can multi-task at a cognitive level, as any busy teacher knows, thinking about several tasks at once. But our cognitive capacity does not allow us to meta-think at the same time. Meta-planning needs our full attention.

Meta-planning can take place at different stages during a learning task:
- before the task, through meta-planning
- during a task, through meta-monitoring
- after the task is completed, through meta-review.

Meta-planning

Encourage able children to think before doing – both at the cognitive level ('What we are we going to do?') and the meta-thinking level ('What do we need to think about?').

Because meta-thinking is about what the children themselves think, it is not enough to tell them what they have previously learnt and what the learning objectives are. We need to help them to think and express these in their own words.

Questions that might help this process include:

- Have you learnt anything like this before?
- What do we need to think about/remember?
- What are we trying to learn today?
- How should we plan it?
- How will you know when you are successful?

Able pupils should be encouraged to put the learning objectives of a lesson in their own words, discuss the learning strategies and identify criteria for success in any given task.

Meta-monitoring

Learners need to monitor their thinking during a task. This means not just asking what they have done, but sharing thinking about how they should be learning. What begins at the shared level through teacher questioning we hope will become internalised as a habit of mind of the child.

Questions that can help this process include:

At the shared level	At the individual level
How are you doing?	How am I doing?
What must you remember?	What must I remember?
What is the process/strategy involved?	What is the process/strategy?
What do you find difficult?	What do I find difficult?
What do you need to think about and do?	What do I need to think about/do?
What will happen if you do this?	What will happen if I do this?
Does it work/make sense?	Does it work/make sense?'

Meta-review

At the end of a task comes the review, plenary or debriefing stage. Review involves reflecting back on your own thinking and learning. (For more on reviewing, see Chapter 9.)

Piaget spoke about the importance of the 'groping and correcting' phase of learning, which is why the monitoring and assessing elements of metacognition are so important. Planning needs to be flexible and strategic, to take account of the unexpected. History is littered with examples of rigid plans that failed, such as Napoleon's march on Moscow in 1812. A specific plan may focus too narrowly on one goal and fail to take account of changes in circumstances. Planning also needs to be personal, to be rooted in what we know and understand, and attuned to our styles of learning and doing.

Teaching planning

Children need to be made aware of planning, to be shown examples of plans and to be given the opportunity to create their own plans. If our aim is to develop independent learners, we need to try to move from teacher-controlled plans to student-controlled planning. This can be achieved in three phases:

1   *Direct instruction phase*
    – explaining to students about plans and planning
    – showing examples of plans and planning strategies
    – involving students in recording/implementing given plans.
2   *Facilitation phase*
    – explaining how plans can be created
    – showing how plans can be modified and extended
    – involving students in putting plans into their own words.
3   *Self-generation phase*
    – explaining that everyone needs to be able to plan
    – showing examples of students' planning
    – involving students in making their own plans.

If planning is essential to success in problem solving and for developing metacognitive skills, then children should have the opportunity to learn about the process of planning and be given experience in planning for specific and strategic purposes. The school curriculum provides the ideal context for introducing the planning process to children. So what contexts can be used for teaching planning?

Using examples from everyday life is the best way to illustrate what planning is, and to bridge the gap between unconscious and conscious mindful planning. One approach is to introduce children from an early age to real-life problems and tasks that require planning.

TASK 14
Planning for problem-solving
1   Identify a real-life problem from your own experience, or ask children to share a problem they have experienced.
2   Share this problem with a child or group of children, expressing the problem at the child's level of understanding.
3   Ask the child (or group) to suggest a plan by which the problem could be solved. Some questions to consider include:
    • What is the action plan? (What steps are needed?)
    • What are the logistics of the plan? (What resources will be needed?)
    • What are the criteria for success of the plan? How will we know if the plan has worked?

I became aware of one approach to teaching about planning during my first year of teaching. One of the problems I faced was what to do first thing on a Monday morning (or at any time when there was nothing timetabled)? At break time I would ask children from other classes what their teachers did. I soon learnt that one young teacher had the problem solved. Every Monday morning she would sit her class down and tell them at least one of the problems she had faced at the weekend or had to face in the week. (Needless to say, she did not, I think, share all her problems.) But her children were fascinated: first, to find out she was human and had problems; and second, that these problems could be shared and talked about. How could she buy something she wanted but could not afford? How should she tile the bathroom? How should she get to know her new neighbours to whom she had never spoken? Whether these problems were real or imaginary, I never discovered, but I knew from the way children would come up to me in the playground and whisper confidentially, 'Do you know what problem she has this week?', that she had found a powerful motivator of interest, and a useful tool for discussing alternative plans of action.

If one way is to discuss plans to overcome problems in the real world, favourite stories are another resource for discussion. Many stories that we share with children have a planning element that can be found in the theme or plot. The following are some questions that could be asked of young children about almost any story that they read or hear:

- What problem(s) did the hero/heroine face?
- What was his/her plan to solve the problem in the story?
- Did the plan work? Why?

An extension of this is to ask children what they would think and do if they were the character in the story. What plan would they try? For example, what plan could they think of if they were one of the three pigs trying to stop the wolf from destroying their house and eating them? Many stories contain a turning point, when a dilemma is faced and a decision is made. These are good moments to pause, and to encourage some thinking time. For example, in the story of Sleeping Beauty when the king and queen know that the princess is under a curse that if she pricks her finger she may die (or sleep for 100 years). What should be their plan? Should they warn their daughter? Is she better-off knowing or not knowing about the curse? What should they do?

Another obvious way of introducing the need for specific planning is the daily programme. What should we do? When should we do it? When should we stop? Why should we do it this way? The child's timetable of activities at school and at home provides good opportunities to discuss the need for forward planning. Research in schools shows that many children do not know what they are going to do in class later that day or later that week. Many have no clear idea of the pattern of their daily activities. The following are some possible timetabling activities for children to plan:

- *daily plan* – record and discuss their planned timetable for the day
- *weekly plan* – record and discuss the planned timetable for the week
- *long-term plan* – record and discuss the major events of the term or year
- *weekend plan* – record and discuss how they plan to spend the weekend (or an ideal weekend)
- *study plan* – record and discuss a timetable for study, such as homework, or study plan for a project
- *holiday plan* – record and discuss their holiday plan
- *life plan* – record and discuss their possible future life plans.

Planning can begin at an early age. The High Scope[8] pre-school/nursery programme for 3–5 year olds has a planning element built in to daily activities. The day begins with the children sitting in a group and each saying what their plan for the morning is, what activities they intend to undertake and in which order. Planning behaviour is reinforced by the expectation that they will collect the apparatus they need from marked storage areas and return the apparatus to the appropriate place. The children are expected to review at the end of the session what they did and how their plan worked. Some young children find planning various activities through a morning quite a challenge. Others learn how to plan for the day, for a week and even longer. They learn that through planning they can bring order, structure and predictability to their world, even if it is just in the prepared environment of the classroom. They are no longer passive recipients of information about what to do, but can be active in planning purposeful activities. If one of the purposes of school is to practise the things you need for life, then practice in planning at any age must be a useful aim of teaching and learning.

TASK 15
Creating a time plan
1 Identify a period of time to plan, for example a day, week, month, half-term, term, year.
2 Show children how activities can be created on a timetable. For example, what would be the timetable for their class in an ideal school?
3 Ask children to:
  a) identify a purpose for their time plan
  b) record their planned activities for the chosen period of time.
  c) present and discuss their finished plans.

Children do not need to plan every activity. Part of learning to plan is to know when planning would be helpful. Opportunities to plan exist in, and can enrich, every area of the curriculum.

Any sequence of activities that make up a lesson is a plan, and can be introduced by saying, 'The plan for this lesson is . . .' A plan should not merely be a set of directions or instructions which tell children to perform one action after another. A plan should include some reference to the process of thinking and learning. The planning process should include some reference to thinking about, monitoring or assessing the outcome of the task.

Figure 3.2 illustrates a plan for learning how to spell a word. It shows an example of a child making the plan his own, after discussion with the teacher, and adding his own drawings.

The features of good plans

There are a number of features characteristic of well-formulated plans. The unconscious, undifferentiated plans used in everyday life may only include a goal and some general idea how to achieve it. These are rarely written down, seldom contain specific details of how to proceed and are not open for others to follow. A well-formulated plan provides a framework which enables people to think through future actions. It helps to organise and structure understanding, and assist us in undertaking practical tasks. A good plan, such as the one illustrated in Figure 3.2, contains a number of important features. These include:

- *Focusing* – Where to start? How to start? – 'Look', 'Say'.
- *Acting* – What to do? In what sequence? – 'Cover', 'Write'.
- *Monitoring* – Is the plan working? What do we need to remember? – 'Think'.
- *Evaluating* – Is the task completed? Has the plan worked? – 'Check'.

It is important that plans provide a starting point. A clear beginning or *focus* shows students where to start, and how to start and what to do, what steps or *actions* to take. The aim of the plan is to liberate the student from direct teacher assistance. Plans are not only a teaching device but aim to provide a means for independent learning. A good plan contains an action component and a thinking component. Good plans needs *monitoring*, which involves thinking (metacognitive) steps to help students in making judgements about what they are doing and intend to do. Without the monitoring and *evaluation* stages, a plan can remain just a set of directions for a given task. A good plan is strategic, and includes skills that can be applied in a number of contexts.

Figure 3.2 A child's plan illustrating 'Look, Cover, Think, Write, Check'

A strategic plan should encompass the FAME formula (focus, act, monitor, evaluate), but may not necessarily have only these four steps. Some plans may include many more steps, such as two focusing, three acting, and so on. In some plans, a step may have a dual function, for example acting and monitoring, or monitoring and evaluation may be just one step. Too many steps make the plan confusing. A useful task is for the teacher to do a model plan in great detail, and ask children to try to simplify the steps in their own words. Keep in mind the magic number seven (plus or minus two) as the ideal number of steps in a finished plan.

Once children gain understanding of the process of planning, and have used plans for a number of purposes, they will become more proficient and confident in planning. They will be able to draw on knowledge of past planning experience to guide them in future planning. As children become more independent learners and problem solvers, they will develop planning skills in the following four areas:

- knowledge of what plans are, and experience in using plans
- skill in formulating plans for different purposes
- understanding when planning would or would not be useful and appropriate
- the disposition to plan and to be strategic in undertaking tasks and solving problems.

Opportunities for planning

Planning works best when it meets student needs. One need that all face in school is the need to communicate through writing. All writing requires planning, or some form of mental rehearsal. Planning can be important in the pre-writing stage.

Another common language activity is book reviewing. Generally students will produce more thoughtful reviews if thought has been given to the process of reviewing and some planning of the elements of a good review have taken place.

Plans can be used in a variety of ways: before attempting a task, during the task or after a task is completed. Plans can be created individually, in pairs, small groups or as a whole class. Plans can serve a variety of purposes, for example:

- Make a plan to help you . . .
- Make a plan to help your group . . .
- Make a plan to help others . . .
- Make a plan to show how you did it
- Make a plan to show others how to do it.

All areas of teaching provide opportunities for planning. The following is a list of some of the possible opportunities for planning in different subject areas:

- *language* – plans for activities in reading, writing, speaking and listening
- *maths* – plans for solving problems, to show working methods and procedures
- *science* – plans of investigations and experiments
- *technology* – plans for designing and making
- *history* – historical plans, such as battle plans, plans for historical research
- *geography* – plans for field trips, plans for geographical research

- *art* – plans for art projects
- *music* – plans for performing, composing or appreciating music
- *physical education* – plans for gymnastics, dance and sports sequences
- *religious education* – plans of religious festivals, rituals, customs, etc., and for research.

All research, whether it is an industrial or university research team, or research undertaken by children at home or school, can benefit from planning. A useful first step in any research activity can be to ask some key questions. The following task provides some questions to help in planning research:

TASK 16

Planning for research

On a chosen topic list, or ask students to list, under three headings:
- What do we know (about the topic)?
- What do we need to know?
- How can we find out? (Where? Who might help us?)

Many practical activities around the school can provide opportunities for planning and problem solving, for example preparing for a class outing, a class presentation, party or fundraising activity. Older students can be asked to plan their homework schedules, and to provide plans for important elements of coursework. Children can be encouraged to talk about their own plans, such as plans for family holidays, plans for winning games, or plans on how to make friends. Figure 3.3 is an example of a child's plan for painting a picture.

My plan for painting a picture

1   Look at the subject you are going to paint. Think about the dimensions, sizes and colours of each part. Take into view the distances and shapes and weigh them up in your head.

2   Roughly sketch the scene in charcoal or dark pencil. Check your sketch and compare it with the scene. Make sure you are happy with each line, for this is the skeleton of your picture.

3   Look carefully at your colours and prepare the paints in your palette. Use the right amount of paint for the style of your painting, but don't use too much.

4   Now start blocking in the basic colours. Slowly but surely work your way round the picture adding details and remembering to do the background first. After a while it is a good idea to stand back from your painting and view your work so far.

5   By now you should have covered the whole page with paint and begin on the details. If you are doing a landscape or seascape, think about putting a few birds in of a few boats, maybe even a couple of people. Just use your imagination. If you are doing a portrait or a still-life, you could perhaps add highlights or shadows.

6   When you have finished your picture stand back and look at it to make sure everything is to your satisfaction.

Figure 3.3 A child's plan for painting a picture

Planning does not ensure success, but it does increase the likelihood of success. At the very least it encourages 'mindfulness'.[9] Mindfulness is the mindset of awareness of the processes we are engaged in. It is seeing the 'big picture', being aware of the context, being open to new information, being focused not just on the outcome but on the process. It is the opposite of mindlessness, the unthinking response, living on 'auto-pilot', being so fixed on the outcome we are no longer aware of the process or context thus unaware of potential hazards or new opportunities. It is what Josh, aged 10, described as 'sort of being awake but not thinking, you're awake but still sleeping, like when you walk into a lamppost.' To be mindless is to be fixed on one idea. As Elaine, aged nine, said, 'Sometimes you have only one thought and you don't have any others and you can only think of that one thought.' A mindless plan is one that is rigid, fixed and has control over what we do. A mindful plan is flexible, open to change and puts the planner in control. It entails multivariable thinking, being aware of the alternatives, open to potential and to creative change. Mindful plans are provisional, flexible and open to creative change. As Christina, aged 11, put it: 'A plan is only yours if you can change it.'

Planning is a fundamental skill for learning and for life and should be part of the daily experience of all children, as it is of all teachers. 'Plans help me to think things through,' said 9-year-old Leila.

Have you made any good plans today?

Summary

Planning is a key process for effective learning and problem solving. Children need help in making use of different types and levels of planning. The ability to plan, particularly strategic planning, helps the metacognitve control of learning. Important aspects of the planning process involve monitoring and evaluation. If planning is important, it should be part of the daily experience of children, infusing all areas of the curriculum. The teaching of planning should be structured so that it moves from teacher-generated planning, to students being more effective in making their own plans. Planning can play a part in all curriculum areas, and is an important part of being 'mindful' in learning and in life.

4 Talking to learn

Talking to learn through dialogue and discussion

As civilised human beings, we are the inheritors, neither of an enquiry about ourselves and the world, nor of an accumulating body of information, but of a conversation, begun in the primeval forests and extended and made articulate in the course of centuries. It is a conversation which goes on both in public and within each of ourselves . . . And it is this conversation which, in the end, gives place and character to every human activity and utterance.
Michael Oakeshott

You don't know what you know until you say it.
James, aged 9

James is a quiet boy. In a class of lively 9 year olds, he can be easily overlooked. As a rather isolated and undemonstrative child, his abilities could easily be under-estimated. He strives in a group to be invisible. But sometimes, as in this lesson, his conversation flowers. It was a discussion in a Philosophy for Children class, talking about whether the brain is the same as the mind. 'You know a lot of things', said James, 'but you don't know what you know until you say it.'

His argument seemed to be that there were many things, items of knowledge and such-like, stored in the brain which you only knew about if you brought them to mind. Sometimes this 'bringing to mind' occurs in dreams, sometimes in thoughts and sometimes in speaking. Much of our knowledge is tacit. Once articulated this knowledge no longer simply resides in tacit form. When articulated it is no longer what Whitehead called 'inert knowledge'. When it becomes available for inspection, it is available for performing a variety of tasks. This 'bringing to mind' through talk can be a powerful thinking and learning strategy. It is part of the long tradition of Socratic teaching, which begins from a seeming ignorance and proceeds through dialogue to a revealed understanding. The Socratic quest of philosophical inquiry through questioning and self-questioning can be seen as a method for getting at personal meanings that may otherwise remain hidden. Socrates, like James, believed that we know more than we know. We may only be dimly aware of the nexus of meanings within which we operate. We may not know what we think until we hear what we say. This perhaps underlies the Delphic injunction 'Know thyself', a process that is served by thought and talk.

This chapter will consider some of the links between talk and thought, from the ego-centric talk of the young child, through different forms of dialogue, to ways of talking to learn through discussion in a classroom community of enquiry.

Talk and thought

There has been much debate among philosophers and psychologists into the relation-ship between thought and language.[1] Does thinking determine language, or does language determine thought? Or is there an interactive relationship between the two? Verbal thinking can be regarded as the internalisation of speech. But the structure of our thinking in a typical conscious thought does not seem to mirror the patterns of fully voiced speech. Vygotsky argues that a better approximation to verbal thought lies in egocentric speech. When children, or adults, talk to themselves about what they are planning or doing, their egocentric speech captures something of the function of thinking. Consider the following from James Joyce's *Ulysses*:[2]

> *. . . that lovely fresh plaice I bought I think I'll get a bit of fish tomorrow or today is it Friday yes I will with some blancmange with blackcurrant jam like long ago not those 2lb pots of mixed plum and apple from the London and Newcastle Williams and Woods goes twice as far only for the bones I hate those eels cod yes I'll get a nice piece of cod . . .*

and compare it with the following from a 5-year-old:

> *I'm going to make a . . . now what do I want. Let's see . . . I'll start with this and fix it on . . . like this. Is it right? It's got to go up . . . wait and see. Brrrrrm! It needs some more . . . not that one. OK what's next? It's got to look right . . .*

As with thinking, egocentric speech has a self-directed regulative function in which the child seeks to represent and respond to the world. As Vygotsky says:[3]

> *the function of egocentric speech is similar to that of inner speech: it does not merely accompany the child's activity; it serves mental orientation, conscious understanding; it helps in overcoming difficulties; it is speech for oneself, intimately and usefully connected with a child's thinking.*

TASK 17

Talking and thinking: a discussion plan

Discuss with a group of children the relationship between talking and thinking. The following are examples of questions that can form the basis of a discussion plan:

- When you talk, do you always think first about what you are going to say?
- Can you talk to someone without thinking?
- Do you ever talk without thinking?
- Which comes first, thinking or talking?
- Is thinking just talking to yourself?
- Can you think without words?
- Can you talk without words?
- Which can you do more quickly, talking or thinking?
- Do you ever talk to yourself? Why?
- Does talking with others help you think and learn? Sometimes? Always? Never? Why?

From an early age, children are busily engaged in creating meaning out of what William James called 'the great buzzing blooming confusion of the world'. They begin to develop 'theories' about what they know and experience. These ideas become the basis of their actions and responses and are tested, validated, revised or improved in the light of subsequent experience. They help the child to anticipate, comprehend events, and to create order out of what would otherwise seem to be random and inexplicable. If this meaning-making capacity is adequate, and subject to testing against reality, then they can achieve competence in their lives. The relationship between the inner world of mind and the outside world becomes creative. Our competence in solving a mathematical problem, painting a picture or maintaining a personal relationship depends on this capacity to construct meanings, from the interaction of ourselves and our environment. Inadequate meanings lead to inadequate responses, to poor levels of anticipation and an inability to comprehend the consequences of ideas and actions. Socrates summed this point up succinctly when he said: 'The unexamined life is not worth living.'

Modelling – recreating the world in words

One way to help this construction of understanding is to talk with ourselves about our experiences, to model the world as we undestand it in words. Vocalisation gives substance to thinking. More accurately, this is sub-vocalisation, for the words do not need to be audible. As adults this 'talking things through' to oneself may seem a natural enough activity. We do not have to see Shakespeare's *Hamlet* to know the experience of a 'stream of consciousness' soliliquy. For children, at the early stages of self-awareness, it is an experience to be encouraged. Teachers can encourage this process by modelling it themselves, by talking things through aloud or as a soliliquy. Examples of this include:

- *Defining the problem* – saying what the situation is, where you are and where you hope to get to, asking questions like: What is the situation? What do I want to achieve? What obstacles prevent me from doing it?
- *Planning a course of action* – talking through a step-by-step approach to a problem, outlining what one hopes to achieve and the stages one hopes to go through. We know from research that a key factor that differentiates experts from novices in most fields of activity is that experts spend more time at the planning stage. Part of the skill of planning is predicting the consequences of an action. Questions in the planning process include: Where/how do I start? What do I need to do? What will happen if I do this?
- *Monitoring the situation* – checking the progress of a plan, action or experience, asking for example: How am I doing? Is it working as expected? What needs doing/thinking about? What should happen next?
- *Reviewing the outcome* – verifying that the task has been achieved, testing the result by asking: Is it finished? Does it make sense? Have I achieved what I set out to do?

In sports coaching, much stress has been placed on the value of the 'inner game', in the belief that planning, anticipating and framing models of play in our head will help improve subsequent performance. Developing the inner game through self-conversation is just one way to do it. As one child reported, 'I like talking things through to myself – no-one interrupts!' It helps the child not only in 'coming to know', but also in their knowledge of themselves – the skills of metacognition (see page 10).

Successful learners have metacognitive skills that involve developing an awareness of their own learning. If children are made aware of their own learning, then they are in a better position to improve it. By modelling examples of talking things through, we can show children ways in which they too can articulate their ideas. We learn to find

ɔy questioning ourselves, and talking through what we have done, what we
and what we hope to do. This self-questioning is in a sense the first stage of
ɔuᴄ. ᴅialogue. If we are to invite children into the club of critical thinkers, we need
to share with them our own thinking processes, and also invite them to share in the
thoughts of others – through dialogue.

Thought and dialogue

Wittgenstein argued that the limits of one's language are the limits of one's world, and
as far as our verbal intelligence is concerned he is surely right. 'Whereof one cannot
speak', he wrote, 'thereon one must remain silent.'[4] As the work of Luria and Yudovich[5]
shows in their classic study of identical twins, creating a social context where dialogue
takes place and where children are persuaded to make their meanings public and therefore explicit produces gains in thinking and learning. From an early age, the boy twins
had developed a private language of their own (a restricted form of Russian), which
could not be understood by their teacher or classmates when, at the age of 5 years, they
went to school. Their play and social understanding was as limited as their speech. The
less backward twin was put in an ordinary class, and after 6 months his language had
improved to the average level expected of the class. The more backward twin was given
in addition a carefully mediated programme during which was forced to articulate his
meaning and understanding. This boy made even more spectacular progress, out performing his brother in both verbal and non-verbal intelligence tests.

Children need opportunities not only to inquire into their own views and ways of
thinking, but also through dialogue with others to discover different perspectives and
points of view. It is through dialogue (as well as through other symbolic means such as
the written word, art, dance, music, etc.) that the private world of the self is extended,
and we are able to overcome the egocentricity of thought by being helped to find more
reflective and considered ways of thinking. Through dialogue, inner speech is turned
into a shared event, what Harri-Augstein[6] has called a 'learning conversation', and
what others have referred to as 'conferencing'.[7]

A learning conversation can be structured around any event or experience. What differentiates a learning conversation, or conference, from day-to-day chat and routine
conversation is that it involves higher-order thinking and raises the process of learning
into awareness. A learning conversation contributes to understanding, it involves
helping children to express their understanding about what they are doing. A learning
conversation therefore involves some form of positive cognitive intervention. It does not
leave everything as it is. It challenges and invites response. The teacher becomes, in a
Socratic sense, a 'gadfly', challenging the *status quo* of a student's thinking by asking
them to express their personal understanding of the topic in hand.

The following are some examples of strategies teachers can use to encourage students
to articulate their thinking through dialogue, and encourage them to become participants in a process of enquiry:

- *Defining the purposes of the activity*, for example by discussing: 'Why are you doing
  this? What do you hope to achieve? How will it help (for example, to fulfil your
  needs/ambitions, or the needs of others)?'

- *Inviting views or opinions* about the topic in hand, for example by asking: 'What do you think? What are your views/opinions/beliefs about the topic? Do you agree with what has been said?'

- *Questioning* the text or topic, to encourage self-monitoring of understanding, for example by asking: 'What do you not know or understand about it? What do you want to find out? What questions can you ask about it?'

- *Clarifying* to help students express what they mean, for example by asking: What does that word/point/detail mean? Can you explain it? Are you saying that . . .?

- *Summarising* to check understanding of the whole of the topic, for example by asking: 'What was said? Can you say it in a few/your own words? Can you say what you think/know?'

- *Developing strategies and tactics*, for example by discussing: 'How can you succeed/do well? What problems/obstacles do you face? What ways can you try (to succeed/overcome problems)?'

- *Evaluating outcomes*, for example by discussing: 'Have you succeeded? What is good about what you have done? What could be improved?'

- *Reviewing the whole process*, for example by discussing: 'Would you do this again? Would you do it this way? What have you learnt from doing it?'

Any learning activity consists of a number of sub-events out of which the whole experience develops. There is, therefore, a double focus to any activity or dialogue, the parts (separate instances, events, experiences, actions, ideas, etc.) and the experience or topic as a whole. So dialogue needs to focus on both general principles and particular examples. It needs to provide insight into parts (analysis), and an overview of the whole (synthesis). One of the advantages of group discussion is that it offers the possibility of including a variety of viewpoints, of exploring the particular individual views of students, as well as the general or organising principles that help to make sense of the topic as a whole. Discussion provides an opportunity to learn what others think, and to express and clarify our own thinking. Discussion can be a powerful vehicle for learning – but what is it, and how should we use it in the classroom?

What is discussion?

The word 'discussion' has two common uses. The first is as a general term to cover a wide range of informal situations where talk occurs between people. According to one researcher,[8] there are more than a dozen forms of discussion, including debate, panel forum, buzz groups and peer tutoring. The second use has a more specific meaning. This refers to a particular form of group interaction where members join together to address a question of common concern, exchanging different points of view in an attempt to reach a better understanding of the issue. This form of discussion has also been called a 'community of enquiry'[9] and it is this ancient and essential educative activity of interpretation or enquiry discussion that will be explored.[10]

Certain conditions can be identified as necessary for a discussion to take place. These include a subject or topic to be discussed, people to discuss it, and certain language or behaviour to facilitate the discussion. If the discussion is to be a genuine process of enquiry, it should reflect certain defining conditions, moral dispositions and intellectual principles.

The central function of discussion is the improvement of knowledge, understanding and/or judgement ... Discussion differs from the social art of conversation in that what the talk is about is a matter of some serious importance.[11]

Defining conditions

Certain characteristics or logical conditions define discussion. These are the conditions that have to be met for us to say that people are actually engaged in discussion. They include that people participating in a discussion must:

- talk to one anther
- listen to one another
- respond to what others say
- consider more than one point of view on the topic under discussion
- intend to develop their knowledge, understanding or judgement on the issue.

Questions that can be used in assessing whether genuine discussion has taken place include:

- Have children talked to one another?
- Have they listened to each other?
- Have they responded to what others have said?
- Have they considered different viewpoints?
- Have they shown development of knowledge, understanding or judgement?

These conditions define what discussion is, but they are matters of degree. All discussion must involve some form of interaction, but in the classroom these conditions can be seen to develop and improve over time, for example by students talking more, listening more attentively, responding more to what others say, putting forward more divergent points of view and being able to correct and refine their judgements.

Moral dispositions

Certain moral principles underlie the successful working of group discussion. Without a moral framework, group discussion cannot function. The moral principles that make discussion possible include:

- *orderliness* – by observing the rules of discussion such as 'only one person speaks at a time', not interrupting or shouting someone down
- *reasonableness* – whereby individuals are willing to listen to the reasons, evidence and arguments of others, and are willing to allow the arguments of others to influence their views
- *truthfulness* – speaking what they believe to be true, not deliberately lying, deceiving others or pretending to believe what they do not believe
- *freedom of expression* – being free to express an opinion, not subject to the restraint by the views of others, by being ridiculed or embarrassed

- *equality of opportunity* – with all having equal access to opportunities to speak and to have the attention of others, not having to suffer the dominance of the few
- *respect for others* – respect for the rights and opinions of others, giving attention and thought to what they say, responding with care and respect for them as persons
- *open-mindedness* – being open to the views of others, willing to change one's mind, being sensitive to the views of others, and willing to suspend judgement.

Ideally we would want children to identify these 'rules for a good discussion' for themselves and to express them in their own words. (For more on developing a community of enquiry, see page 54.)

If classroom discussion reflects moral principles and dispositions such as these, then it will help to foster the intellectual qualities or virtues of participants. If students and teachers exhibit these attitudes and concerns during the course of discussion, they will grow in these qualities and become a model for others. The cultivating of understanding will be enhanced by being responsive to the opinions of others, by being reason-seeking in argument, reflective in judgement, and by communicating in clear, concise and consistent fashion. These intellectual virtues play a vital role in the search for meaning and order in a confusing world. They help strengthen the ability to make reasonable judgements about what to think and do.

TASK 18
Why use discussion?
What are your views on the use of discussion?
The following questions about the use of discussion could help frame your own thinking, or act as a starting point for discussion with colleagues or students.
 1 What is a discussion?
 2 Is every kind of talking together a discussion?
 3 Do discussions need rules? If so, what should they be?
 4 What good can come out of discussing things with others?
 5 What do you like/not like about discussions?
 6 Can you remember a good discussion? (What made it good?)
 7 What things are best for discussion?
 8 Are there some things you would not want to discuss?
 9 Do you prefer to talk or listen in a discussion?
10 What would you like to discuss?

Teaching through discussion

There has been much research in recent years into ways teachers generate talk with and between children.[12] Close attention has been given to the use of talk in the classroom, often involving the analysing of evidence on tape. This has highlighted the value of exploratory talk, of talking round, talking through and talking about topics of study, as well as the importance of having a purpose and an audience for talk. Talk needs to be directed to an end, towards a question or focus of enquiry, or as part of a learning conversation. Talk for its own sake may be congenial, but it is often unproductive, as the idle chatter of children in unsupervised groups often shows. But the tapes and observations of teachers also revealed ways in which teachers sometimes negated their purpose of supporting learning through talking.

Teachers confirmed what much research into classroom interaction had suggested, that in their conversations teachers took up more talking time than children. The recommended intervierwer:interviewee ratio of talk should, it is said, be about 20:80, but teachers often find themselves not providing good models for discussion. 'I heard myself dominating the discussion', said one teacher, 'interrupting children, asking questions and rephrasing answers, and, worst of all, not listening to what they said.'[13]

In classroom discussion, children tend to talk directly to the teacher, competing for attention, or become monosyllabic in their responses. They become dominated by the need for approval, rather than by the search for understanding. They tend to be fearful of taking risks, inhibited from exploring the unfamiliar or from building on the ideas of others – all aspects of talk that needs to be developed if children are to fully explore their ideas. This is partly due to the standard forms of classroom discourse, where the teacher takes on the role as the provider of answers and the dispenser of approval. Such established patterns are hard to alter, but in building a genuine community of enquiry, there is a need to make explicit any changes that are being made in the 'educational ground rules'.[14]

The ground rules for 'talking to learn' should include the teacher making clear their role in the learning situation.

Teacher as expert

There are many situations where teachers need to take on the role of expert, sustaining the attention of individuals or groups, leading pupils to higher levels of understanding through direct teaching methods. This means 'scaffolding' the steps to learning and understanding so that students achieve their optimum potential in assisted learning or performance. This may be achieved for example by explaining, by questioning or by demonstration.

Teacher as facilitator

Teachers often organise situations where children are working in groups. In this role the teacher has a management function rather than a direct teaching role. The children may be free to explore ideas and to help each other in a collaborative venture without constant reference to the teacher, although the teacher may intervene when pupils don't seem to be getting on. Students can benefit from working collaboratively without teacher intervention, and can become skilled at managing group interactions, for example ensuring that each in the group has a turn.

It is helpful if groups have had a chance to establish and agree the ground rules for discussion beforehand. The following are some rules agreed by a class of 11-year-olds:

- Listen to what other people say.
- Be kind to each other and give support.
- Think before you speak or ask a question.
- Be polite, and don't laugh at what other people say.
- Respect others – if people don't want to say anything they don't have to.

Open questions and dilemmas can be as fruitful in stimulating discussion and argument. These can be generated from news items in the papers or on TV, from the lives
of children (for example, having a 'problem' or 'help box' where children can anonymously post problems for later discussion), or from open questions of a general nature.

Examples of open questions to stimulate discussion include:

- What is bullying? What should be done about it?
- Is it more important to be rich or happy?
- Is it better to be an adult or child?
- Are boys and girls treated differently? Should they be?
- What is a hero? Who are your heroes? Why?
- What are laws? Why are they needed? (Create a set of laws for a fictitious society.)
- Should children be smacked if they are naughty?

One way to facilitate discussion is to have a ranking activity in which groups are given
cards on which statements are written. The group is asked to discuss and rank them in
order of importance, for example in a triangle or diamond (Figure 4.1), with the most
important at the top.

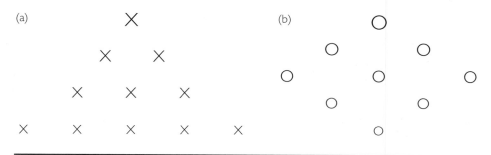

Figure 4.1 Two ways of ranking: (a) in a triangle, (b) in a diamond

For example, after a class had discussed the question 'What is a friend?', the teacher
gave out the following statements about friendship and asked them to sort the statements into two piles, one for those they agreed with and one for those they disagreed
with. Each group then compared their decisions with another group, and then with
the whole class:

- A friend is someone who is always there to help when things go wrong.
- A friend will always forgive you if you do something wrong.
- Friends are just the people you see every day.
- Friends are people who are the same race and religion as you.
- A friend is someone who does what you say.
- A friend is someone who will never lie to you.
- A friend is a special person you can share secrets with.
- A friend is someone who is loyal to you – no matter what.

Teacher as participant

Discussion between pupils can often be useful, but talk for learning is generally enhanced by the active participation of a teacher or experienced adult. The benefits that a teacher can bring to an inquiry or learning conversation include the following elements of mediation:

- *focusing* – by directing attention to important points, issues or factors
- *seeking meaning* – by asking for reasons, explanation or clarification
- *expanding* – by showing links between ideas, and links to new ideas
- *rewarding* – by verbal or non-verbal expressions of positive response.

One of the purposes of teacher as participant is to get pupils to talk and listen to each other, rather than directing all their talk through the teacher. The aim is to help children to feel independent and equal in their responses to each other, and to create what Lipman calls 'a community of enquiry'.[15]

Community of enquiry

A community of enquiry is a teaching method that includes the following elements:

- *community setting* – where all can see/hear each other, in a circle or horseshoe
- *agreed rules* – discussed and presented for all to see and remember
- *shared stimulus* – a focus for discussion such as question, issue, text, picture or video
- *thinking time* – time to think silently, to share thinking with partner or small group
- *questions* – children suggest questions, which are written for all to see
- *discussion* – A question is chosen and discussed by the group.

During discussion, the role of the teacher is to focus the group's attention on the question or issue under discussion, and to push for depth by posing further questions, asking for reasons and evidence and by presenting alternative viewpoints. The aim is to encourage serious, systematic and sustained attention on the question or issue in hand. Asking open or Socratic questions (see below) is one way to probe thinking, but alternatives to questions can be just as effective in challenging and extending thinking.

In discussion with children we need to be consistent in our behaviour, for example by:

- encouraging participation by valuing and appreciating the contributions of all children
- displaying patience and listening seriously and carefully to what they say
- building on ideas and pushing for depth in discussion
- expecting reasons and explanation for what children believe and say
- ensuring that all honour the group's agreed rules for discussion.

Extending the discussion

One of the problems in class discussion is the brevity of many children's responses. Discussion is sustained when extended responses from children are expected, encouraged and supported. Discussion leaders need to help children to build on their own and others' ideas, express them fully, consider a range of viewpoints and reach common understandings. This can happen through talk with an individual child, in pairs or small groups or in whole class discussion.

Effective discussion depends on the quality of questioning and the use of alternatives to questions (see page 25). Some strategies that help extend thinking in a discussion include:

- *Wait time* – allow five seconds or more thinking time, before and after a response.
- *Think–pair–share* – individual thinking time, then discussion with a partner, then group.
- *Ask for more* – make a non-verbal or verbal invitation to say more.
- *Withhold judgement* – respond in a non-judgemental way, for example 'Thank you'.
- *Cue alternatives* – ask, for example: Who agrees/disagrees?, Who has another view?
- *Challenge the response* – ask 'Why?' or offer a different viewpoint.
- *Make a personal contribution* – offer more information, your own experience or ideas.
- *Invite their further contributions* – ask if anyone has a question to ask or idea to share.

A group of 10 year olds have read a story and are sitting in a circle discussing Joanne's question: 'Why are there good and bad people?' They are used to this format and listen attentively to each other. A number of different opinions are expressed. No one feels nervous about sharing their own opinions or questioning the opinions of others. There are periods when many want to speak at once, and times of quiet reflection. The teacher guides her students to consider their thoughts in greater depth and to give reasons for their views. This is an extract from that discussion:[16]

Child: I think people are basically good and want to do good things.
Teacher: Anyone agree or disagree with that?
Child: I disagree with Jane. I think everyone has bad within them. It is only parents or teachers who make you good.
Child: I think we are born good but it is things like television that make you bad. Seeing bad things gives you bad ideas.
Child: I think people are both good and bad. There's good and bad in everyone, just waiting to come out really. That's how we are made. You can choose to be good or bad.
Teacher: What do you think helps you to be good?
Child: It's your feelings really. If you do good things, you feel good.
Child: Sometimes when you do bad things, you feel good too!
Teacher: Can you give an example of that?
Child: Like taking ice cream when you shouldn't.
Child: I think there is a difference. When you are doing good things for others, like helping an old lady across the road, you are feeling for them. When you do bad and selfish things you are only feeling for yourself.

At the end of the discussion, it can be helpful to review the discussion, the children's thinking, the views and ideas of others and what they have learnt (for more on review, see page 121). Activities and exercises may be used to extend thinking about a key issue, developing skills of self-expression through art and drama, and other forms of creative expression. An extension activity might be to make a 'mindmap' of the main points in the discussion (see Chapter 5) or give students their own 'thinking book', journal or learning log to write and record their reflections after the enquiry.

All areas of the curriculum can provide opportunities for learning conversations and contexts for discussion.[17]

TASK 19

Contexts for discussion

What are the possible contexts for encouraging discussion in the classroom?

1 Make a list of possible opportunities for discussion within the curriculum where talk may help thinking and learning.
2 What is the role of the teacher in leading discussion?
3 Consider the contexts for discussion under three headings:
   - Teacher as expert
   - Teacher as facilitator
   - Teacher as participant.

Socrates was called a 'midwife of ideas' – and this is an apt description of any teacher who seeks to develop talk for learning. Talking to learn can be considered to be an aspect of cognitive apprenticeship. Key elements in this process include:

- *modelling* – demonstrating self-questioning and the articulation of ideas;
- *coaching* – facilitating the articulation and questioning of ideas through dialogue;
- *practice* – providing opportunities for talking and learning in communities of enquiry.

The following dialogue is an extract from a community of enquiry with a group of 11-year-old children. After raising several questions from the reading, one was chosen for discussion: 'Is your brain the same as your mind?'

RF: Is your brain the same as your mind? Let's see if we can get a bit closer to an understanding of that. Tom, why did you ask that question?

Tom: Well is it . . . I mean your brain controls your heart and your arms and everything that goes on in your body, but does your mind really think, 'Okay, I'll move left,' and do you think 'Okay brain send messages down to the muscles to move'?

RF: So are you saying because the brain has its messages that the mind is not aware of that it means that the mind cannot be the same as the brain?

Tom: Yes, it isn't the same as the brain, because it's part of the brain but it isn't the brain.

   [*This age-old question in philosophy prompted a number of comments from children, agreeing, disagreeing, suggesting or building on ideas . . .*]

Child: I think I'd agree with Tom that your mind is part of the brain. But . . . if you'd like to put one inside the other you'd put the mind inside the brain.

RF: So if the mind is inside the brain . . .

Tom: Or inside part of it . . .

RF: Part of it. How do you think it's different from the brain. If not the same as the brain, it must be different, mustn't it?

Tom: Well, the brain controls everything about us, the mind as well, but the mind only controls our thoughts . . . and contains our thoughts.

Child: Memory . . .

Tom: I think the mind is made out of memories and thoughts . . . it's a thinking bank.

RF: So, is the mind the same as the brain, but the brain just bigger than the mind? Or is the mind different from brain?

Child: Different.

Child: Yes.

Child: Because it doesn't control anything . . . the mind just thinks.

Child: The mind, I think, is our thoughts more than controlling our body. I mean, our brain sends messages everywhere round our body all the time to nerves and everything, or they are sending messages to the brain, but the mind isn't part of this, I don't think. I think the mind just contains your thoughts.

Child: And memories

[*The discussion moved on to what happens when you die . . .*]

Child: I think when your brain dies it's like a shutdown, and it shuts down your body. And I don't think your mind does carry on really, it just shuts down every system and your brain has to work your mind really because I don't think your mind would really work if your brain had shut down.

[*Children went on to discuss what happens in the mind when you dream, and were then encouraged to think of analogies for the mind . . .*]

RF: Would you agree with someone who says the mind is a bit like smoke in the brain – a sort of strange ghost?

Child: Yeah.

Child: Yes.

RF: If it's like a strange ghost, then could it live outside the brain?

Child: Not like a ghost

Child: The mind's not like that . . . it's not very good . . .

RF: Not a good way to describe the mind? A lot of thinking goes on in what are called analogies. We've got to liken it to something else to understand it better. What would you say the mind is like?

Child: Like a big warehouse . . . with things on the back shelves of your memory . . . and things being moved around in your thoughts.

Child: Yeah.

RF: So part of the warehouse is called the mind? The active part . . .

Tom: No, the warehouse is your mind.

[*Discussion continued on how the mind was like a warehouse . . .*]

RF: If the mind is like a warehouse what is the brain like? Can you continue this analogy?

Child: A brain is like a . . . a . . . beehive.

Child: A dock . . . containing lots of different warehouses for doing different things.

Child: An ants' nest!

[*The topic ended with children being offered a 'last word', and the chance to sum up their thoughts . . .*]

RF: So if we come back to Tom's question – 'Is your mind the same as the brain?' – we could now formulate a much better answer to that, couldn't we?

Tom: Yes.

RF: How would you sum up your answer now, Tom?

Tom: Your brain is like a dock and your mind is like a warehouse in it containing all your memories and thoughts on lots of different shelves . . . and your brain sends out different messages around and across the dock.

Talking to learn, as the above transcript shows, is not an exact art. It is a process of learning to think and reason through learning to talk with and to listen to others. The teacher models the process 'teaching by example', and mediates the process by building on what children can contribute and by providing opportunities for enquiry to take place. This exemplary role of the teacher is summed up well in the words of Michael Oakeshott, 'Not the cry, but the rising of the wild duck impels the flock to follow him in flight.'[18]

Summary

Talking and thinking are closely linked in the child's attempts to reflect on and make meaning out of experience. Aspects of talking to learn include talking things through to oneself, dialogue with others and group discussion. The teacher can help children to develop communicative competence through discussing matters that require the exercise of thought and judgement. In such discussions the teacher can act as expert, facilitator or participant. The teacher's role is to extend and sustain classroom discussion. Curriculum activities, and thinking skills approaches such as 'community of enquiry', can provide contexts for discussion and enquiry.

5 Visual tools for learning

Visual tools can help organise thinking and learning.

As any photographer knows, the frame of the viewfinder organises the image within it, creating a visual statement where, without the frame, one might see only clutter. And, as any builder knows, the frame of a building supports its totality. Both metaphors highlight a crucial feature of thinking frames. They support and organise thought, but they do not do the thinking. They are guides, not recipes.

David Perkins[1]

When you make a map, it helps you to think about what you know and what you don't know.

Omar, aged 11

A map is a useful guide to where we are, and where we wish to go. A map is a useful geographical tool. It is a way of making our thinking about space and location visible, showing us the inter-relationships of places. We carry within us many mental maps that help us find our way round the locations we know and locations where we have never been.[2] Maps can be pictorial or made with symbols. (Usually printed maps are both pictorial and symbolic.) Maps can also be made out of words, ideas and concepts. *Cognitive maps*, created by the mind, can be powerful tools for memorising and learning.

What are cognitive maps?

Cognitive maps go under a variety of names: concept maps, semantic maps, knowledge maps, word webs, networks, clustering, mind-maps, think-links, idea branches, structured overviews or graphic organisers.[3] All such processes, which involve the diagramming of thinking, can be called cognitive maps. Cognitive maps attempt to visually and graphically portray a relationship of ideas or concepts. They are sometimes called concept maps because identifying key words and concepts make it easier for us to use language, not only to make study notes but also in thinking, learning and remembering.

How maps develop memory

Memory is primarily a process of making links, connections and associations between new information and existing patterns of knowledge. Memory depends in large part on key words and key concepts which, when properly remembered, are transferred from short-term memory into long-term memory. It is through the linking of information to existing patterns of knowledge that we create new forms of understanding. If we cannot identify key words and concepts, and have not created patterns of understanding, then our understanding and our memory become fragmentary – we have not 'grasped' things, we have not created an effective map. In a sense all our knowledge is fragmentary, our understandings are partial. Like fifteenth-century maps of the world, there may be large areas of ignorance and incomprehension in our understanding of things. However, there are some firm foundations in our knowledge. We can show this by making our thinking visible through words, numbers, pictures, etc., and through mapping concept words. But why concept words? Why not sentences?

We have become so used to speaking and writing in words that we could easily assume that sentence structure is the best way of learning and remembering verbal images and ideas. In recalling information, we rarely use a word-for-word verbatim process, we do not 'reread' from memory what we have learnt. This would be a very long and demanding process. It would be like having to learn and remember playscripts all the time. We are able to access so many memories because all we need is to remember the key ideas, words or images and we recreate what we remember from these. When people describe a story, event or idea, they usually extract the key elements and weave them into a fresh recreation. Exceptions to this are when specific 'scripts' have been learnt, as in joke-telling – though often here memory will rely on key phrases and images, and the tale will vary in the telling. This is why gossip (and many sorts of 'news gathering') is often unreliable in its details; memory is selective and episodic. We can research this with children through the use of memory games.

TASK 20
Memory games
The following games can serve as an investigation and stimulus for thinking about how memory works.

Chinese whispers
1   Put children into some continuous order, such as a circle or line.
2   Whisper a message into the first child's ear, so that others cannot hear.
3   Each child then passes the message they heard to the next child until the message runs from the first to last child.
4   Compare the message that went 'in' to the one that came 'out' at the end of the line.
5   Try messages of different complexity.
6   Discuss why the repeated message might have changed.

Secret stories
1   Go with a child out of the room, and tell a story.
2   A second child goes out of the room to hear the story recounted by the first child.
3   The first child returns. A third child goes out to hear the story from the second child.
4   The second child returns, a fourth goes out, and so on.
5   After a given number of turns, when the last child is out of the room tell the original version, and invite the last child in to tell the last version as she or he heard it.
6   Compare versions and discuss. Are there ways of helping you to remember better?

Creating meaning with concepts

The world is filled with a rich multiplicity of objects and experiences. We make order out of the world through transforming our perceptions (what we see, hear, feel, etc.) into concepts (words and ideas). We are greatly helped in this process by sharing our experiences and ideas with others. A concept is an organising idea, an abstraction that pulls together a lot of facts, attempting to make sense of them by organising them into categories or classes. Concepts help us to classify and order thoughts and experiences, providing the labels that we give to these patterns of ideas. For instance, the scientific taxonomy (category system) for animals on our planet uses concepts such as class, order, family and species to organise our thinking about the creatures we have identified. Concepts group certain facts together to make distinctions and relationships between things. They express patterns of similarities and differences that organise and help to explain experience. They are constructions of the human mind that enable us to make sense and to learn from experience.

Concepts are the labels we give for ideas that may be simple, such as 'dog' and 'cat', or which may have complex layers of meaning, such as 'democracy' and 'revolution'. To understand a concept well, it is not sufficient to be given a dictionary or textbook definition. Many concepts have a variety of definitions which help explain the meaning of the ideas contained in the word. Another key aspect of understanding a concept is to be able to see what is, and what is not, an example of it. Skilled teachers combine these two processes, of giving explanations and examples, with a third process – helping the child to come to a communicative understanding of the concept (see Figure 5.1).

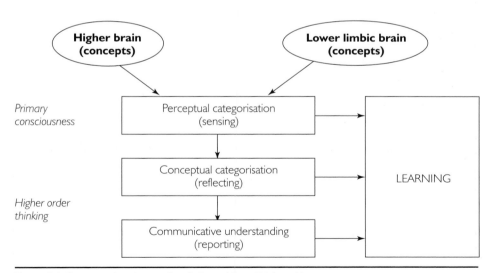

Figure 5.1 Conceptual understanding (adapted from Edelman)[4]

Explanations are important, since children often have an incomplete grasp of what adults mean when they give a label to things. Examples are important as children will often misapply concepts, such as the young child calling geese and swans 'ducks'

LIVERPOOL JOHN MOORES UNIVERSITY
LEARNING SERVICES

because they are duck shaped. We don't know, however, even after careful explanations and examples, whether a concept has been assimilated into a child's wider knowledge of the world until we ask the child to represent and to share what they know. Creating a thinking map (or concept map) is one way of representing and communicating their understanding of concepts.

The understanding of a concept can vary enormously between children. What the concept of a colour or number is to a 3 year old is very different to what it is to a 10 year old. A nursery teacher may talk of a child 'knowing his colours' when he knows, for example, what is green. The older child will have a fuller understanding of what green is, such as that it can be made from yellow and blue, and knows many more examples of 'greenness'. He may know that 'green' is also an abstract term referring to environmental issues. However, his understanding may not be perfect. He may find it difficult to identify green in a painting of the sea, or know that green can be a symbol of jealousy. So learning a concept is not an 'all or nothing' process; it is the building up of successive approximations, of finer distinctions, of a widening network of related ideas, of coming closer to the common understandings of a culture and to the knowledge structure of experts. We increase our understanding by constructing and developing a wider network of meanings.

Linking ideas

We create meaning by making links between words and ideas. We learn more by making more links, by exploring and by testing links. The following task illustrates and provides practice in this process of connecting words and ideas.

TASK 21

Making connections

You may like to try these tasks yourself before trying them with children.

Random words

1 Ask children to suggest any interesting word that comes into their minds.
2 Collect about 12 words, and display them on a board.
3 They think about the words and try to pair up any two words with a linking idea, for example head/hat (hats go on heads).
4 Try to find pairs of words in this way, or trios, for example horse/feet/helicopter (means of transport), or larger sets or families of words. Work individually or with a partner, allow thinking time, share findings with the group. A possible extension is to try to link all the words in an interesting story or explanatory narrative.

Topic words

1 List, or ask children to suggest, the dozen or so most important words on a chosen topic, for example 'Ancient Egypt', 'pond life', 'time'.
2 As above, ask the children to think about the words and try to link them together with a connecting idea or ideas.
3 These can be discussed or displayed in visual form.

'Only connect', said E.M. Forster. Making connections is the way we create an under-standing of the world, and is the basic process of all creative thinking. Are there any two words or concepts that cannot be linked in the mind with some sort of connecting idea? Descartes suggested that if we knew everything there was to know about any-thing, we would have found out everything there was to know about everything. There is a sense in which all knowledge is threads within a seamless robe. We are just not aware of all the hidden links and connections. We are always in a state of incomplete knowledge, of coming to know, of building on our partial understandings. Through-out life, we are (or should be) constantly building on and developing our conceptual understanding of the world.

Concept development and explanation

Vygotsky identified two levels of concept development. The first level is where con-cepts are spontaneously developed through perceptual and practical experience in everyday activity. They are developed through rich experiences, but they are unsys-tematic and relate to particular human contexts. On the higher level are 'scientific' concepts, which are theoretical and structured, and depend on the use of language and learning. Concepts are either:

- *spontaneous* – learned through direct sensory experience such as learning what an orange is through touch, taste, sight etc.; *or*
- *scientific* – abstracted from experience, learned through language, for example that all oranges have certain common elements such as 'roundness'.

'Scientific' or abstract concepts are powerful because they can be applied to different contexts and fields of learning. They can be translated into increased abstraction, awareness and control of thought. These more advanced concepts can easily be cut off from experience and become unconnected with the concepts of everyday life. Hence the need for explanation – explanation from others (learning) and explanation to others (communication). The use of examples can help to embed knowledge in a human context. The use of explanation linked to examples is inductive reasoning and the basis of scientific method.

There are of course different levels of explanation, for example:

- *labelling* – giving no explanation, 'things just are', for example 'this is an orange'
- *enumerating* – giving odd facts, 'this is what they are', for example 'there are oranges in shops'
- *making a link* – pairing contiguous ideas, for example 'oranges grow on trees'
- *identifying common characteristics* – similarities, for example 'oranges are round, orange colour, have pips', etc.
- *identifying concepts belonging to a class* – knowing class names, for example 'oranges are fruit/food'
- *identifying concepts belonging to a pattern or hierarchy* – relating to other classes, for example orange as fruit/food/plant/living thing
- *relating concepts to other patterns of concepts* – identifying similarities/differences

with other classes, for example orange related to linguistic, mathematical, scientific, historical, geographical, economic and other conceptual patterns.

Piaget argued that concepts are organised into 'schemas' or 'models', which are mental representations of things or ideas, and it is through these that we process information. For Piaget, cognitive development was very much to do with conceptual development, and this was often best achieved through cognitive conflict when our existing concepts or 'schemas' are challenged, and our existing ideas disturbed. To learn is to change. Cognitive development must entail some change, some re-arrangement or enlargement of the conceptual structure. It is these conceptual structures that underlie skills and understanding.

Concepts change and become more complex over time, and this process of conceptual development is helped by sharing our understandings and being challenged by the thoughts of others. One way of sharing an understanding of a concept is to list characteristics, and compare, contrast or discuss our ideas with others. For this, any concept can be chosen — one that is in the news, one that is under study, one chosen by a child, and so on. It can be a simple concept like 'tree' or 'wet', or something more complex like 'anger' or 'democracy'.

TASK 22

Listing characteristics

This is best begun as a group or class activity, and later as a paired or individual activity. It presents that most basic of problem-solving strategies — consider all factors, list all characteristics, find out what you know/find out what others know, define the concept.

1　Choose a concept.
2　Write it on a board, large piece of paper or projector.
3　Ask the group to give as many characteristics/definitions as possible of the concept word.
4　List all suggestions.
5　After listing, discuss similarities/differences. Could they be grouped into an order?

Concept mapping

Concept mapping is one way that we can try to make visible a conceptual structure, not simply to see what it is, but to process it, to challenge it and to help enlarge it.

How do you introduce children to the language of concepts? One way is to describe concepts as any word that means something, for example names of people, places, things, events, ideas. It can help to say that a concept is a word that you can picture in the mind, not a linking word like 'and', 'but' or 'here'. We might say that a concept word has some connotation — it means something. Some words have no connotation, they merely act as connectors with other words, for example 'the', 'an', 'and'. It is not always clear what a concept word is, or if a fixed meaning can be given to all, or any, words. Must all concepts be clear and open to definition, or are some concepts 'fuzzy' and never fully defined? Who defines what words or concepts mean? Philosophers have argued about the nature of concepts for centuries. Children too can take part in this discussion, at their own level and for the purpose of coming to their own understanding.

The best way to begin introducing concept maps to children is to construct some of your own, first with general topics such as animals or vehicles, then with topics of study in school. The mapping of a subject should help you to think more clearly about it. When you have practised the process, you may wish to introduce your pupils to the process.

Generating initial concept maps

One way of generating initial concept maps with children is as follows.

1 Ask children to close their eyes and ask them if they can see a picture in their mind when you say a familiar word for an object, such as 'dog', 'chair' or 'grass'. Write these on the board and ask children for more examples.

2 Children now close their eyes and see a picture while you say an event word such as 'raining', 'running' or 'painting'. Ask children for more examples, and write them on the board.

3 Explain that words have meaning for us if we can see them as pictures in the mind. Try a few unfamiliar words to see if they can picture them in the mind. (If you have bilingual pupils, you might try to introduce a few familiar 'foreign' words to show that people use different labels for the same meaning.)

4 Introduce the word 'concept' and explain it is a way of describing a word that can be pictured in the mind. Review some words on the board to see if they are concept words.

5 Write some linking words such as 'the', 'is', 'are', 'when', 'that', 'then'. Ask if these words bring pictures to the mind. Explain that these are not concept words but words that link concepts in sentences. Ask for more examples of linking words.

6 Ask the children to read some sentences from a book and to identify the concept words and linking words.

7 Ask children to pick a concept word, and begin to list information (brainstorm) about the word as a preparation for making their own concept maps.

Listing words and concepts is a useful activity. It encourages fluency and flexibility of ideas, and provides a good basis for writing or for further classification. However, many people find it easier to take in information that is presented in a non-linear form. The brain works in complex patterns, which are integrated and interlinked. We are used to receiving information from the world, from pictures and TV in non-linear visual patterns. In nature there are no straight lines. Some of us prefer to think in straight lines, as observation of suburban gardens and the pattern-making of children show. Others prefer a more organic visual stimulus, rather than traditional 'lines'.

In a concept map (or mind map), a key word or concept is one that is linked to many others, and serves as a focal point for making connections with other parts in the pattern. A key concept in the study of nature might be 'animal', for example, and each of these could be linked to a family of related concepts (see Figure 5.2). A pattern working out from the centre of a main idea has a number of advantages:

- The central, main or key idea is clearly defined.
- The relative importance of ideas can be clearly shown by being highlighted , or put nearer the centre.
- Links between ideas can be clearly shown.
- Visual patterning allows for easy overview and review.
- The structure is provisional and organic, allowing for additions and adaptations.
- The open-ended nature of the process encourages the making of connections between ideas.
- Each pattern is individual and unique, making it easier to remember, recall and repeat.

The first stage is often the brainstorming of ideas and connections. An important feature of thinking maps is that the *connecting ideas* are made explicit, either through discussion or through being written along the line that connects the concept words. It is making connections visible or explicit that differentiates thinking maps from the simple brainstorming of ideas. The process can be an important aid to learning. Once it has been tried in a class or group with others it can become a learning tool to be used whenever needed and for a variety of purposes. What purposes can this think mapping serve?

TASK 23
Thinking maps

Brainstorming
This task is a useful pre-writing or pre-mapping exercise.
1 Choose a concept word, for example 'spiders' and ask children to list all the words they can think of connected to the concept. What words do they list?
2 Compare their list with a partner's list. What words are the same, and different?
3 Share with the whole group.

Concept mapping
1 After brainstorming/listing words connected to a concept, write the concept word in the middle of the board or page.
2 Link the connected words to the central concept word with lines.
3 Write along the lines the relationship between the concept and connected words.

Mapping a text
1 Give each pair of children a page from a reading book or textbook (a text of 10/30 sentences). Ask them to list, or mark, every concept word they can find.
2 How often does the same concept word appear? Which concept word appears most often? Which are the most important concept words? (In other words, which could you not leave out for the passage to still make sense?)
3 List or mark words that are not concepts, which don't mean anything by themselves.
4 Share and discuss.

The purposes of concept mapping

Concept mapping can serve a number of purposes. Three of the main aims or purposes of making thinking visible through cognitive mapping (think-mapping, mind-mapping or concept mapping) are:

- *to explore what we know* – to identify the key concepts, to show links between ideas and to make a meaningful pattern out of what we know and understand[5] (see Figure 5.2)
- *to help planning* – as an aid to planning an activity or project by organising ideas, grouping them and showing links between them (see Figure 5.3)
- *to aid evaluation* – to help the evaluation of experience or knowledge through a process of reflection on the key elements of what we know or have done (see Figure 5.2).

Cognitive maps can provide children with a way to articulate their ideas. They provide a tool for planning and for assessing or evaluating what they know. They stimulate active thinking, develop cognitive skills of analysis, categorisation and synthesis, and provide a visual means for communication and evaluation. A major benefit of mapping is that we can use this practical, visually-oriented strategy within the context of any topic in the school curriculum. There are a number of different map structures (see below) that can help students to represent and organise what they know and can find out. Mapping strategies can allow teachers to cover topics in greater depth, where meanings can be found and created in an organised and ongoing way. A map design can be displayed on a digital whiteboard and be viewed, adapted and developed over time. Software enables children to create their own visual diagrams, ready-made visual organisers that enable them to experiment with ways of presenting information and ideas. Mapping provides a visual framework for thinking and the storing of information which can be added to over time. Mapping provides a learning framework in which all the areas of language skill – speaking, listening, reading and writing, can be used in meaningful ways.

Rather than a passive teaching/learning environment, mapping encourages children to be actively engaged in thinking, to elaborate and build on ideas. They not only receive information, but need to re-think it, interpret it and relate it to their schemas of understanding. Mapping can help information flow to, from and among pupils and teachers. Most importantly, they learn a procedure for investigating and organising information, showing understanding of the relationships between concepts and developing a visual strategy to aid to memory. Learning to organise ideas is an important pre-writing strategy and an important study skill in helping to understand the structure of any text they read. Mapping can be used in all curriculum areas.[6] In addition, with mapping, pupils and teachers have the opportunity to use computers to reinforce the skills both of mapping and of learning curriculum content; because mapping is a highly visual/spatial activity, the whiteboard or personal computer are ideal for displaying networks of visual information. What then are the forms that think mapping can take?

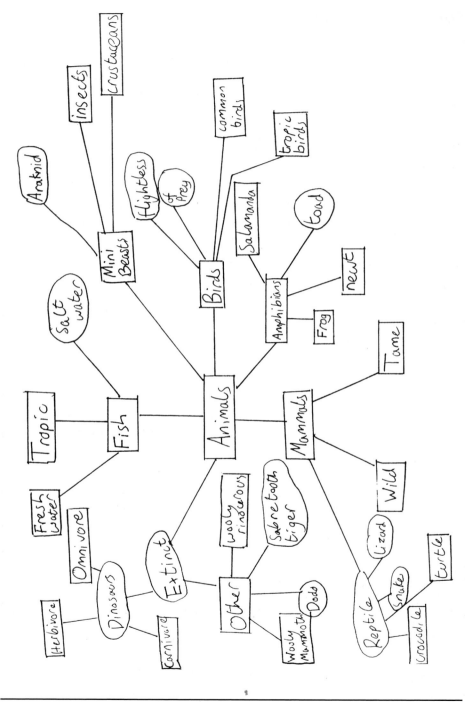

Figure 5.2 A cognitive map of a project about animals

Forms of mapping

A map visually consists of an arrangement of shapes such as boxes, circles, rectangles, triangles, etc. connected by lines and/or arrows drawn between and among the figures. The map conceptually contains verbal information within and between the shapes to create a pattern or relationships of ideas. The aim of the map is to show how the whole topic in question can be portrayed. There are several forms that this mapping can take.

Hierarchical concept mapping

Simple concept maps create a semantic web from a simple idea or key concept. A more advanced strategy is to map concepts into a hierarchical form. A hierarchical concept map shows pupils how to represent a hierarchy of ideas within a given topic and to show the relationships between them. Research shows that children as young as 5 years can create hierarchical concept maps of a simple kind, but it is not usually until around the age of 10 that children produce maps that show quality and complexity of thinking – and it is around this age that some teachers have found group work on hierarchical concept mapping to be most beneficial.

The following tasks help to develop children's understanding of concept mapping.

TASK 24

Hierarchical concept mapping

Listing hierarchies
1 Make a list of 10 or 12 words related to a concept, for example 'seaweed', 'plankton', 'fish', 'shark', 'plants', 'mammals', 'shoals', 'coral', 'whales', 'waves', 'tides', 'currents'.
2 Ask children to name the concept that relates to all the words, for example 'sea'.
3 Build a concept map by organising the concept words from the more general to the more specific concepts in a visual hierarchy.
4 Ask children to add words, and show cross links if they can.

Creating hierarchical maps
1 List words on a chosen concept, for example 'dogs'. Ask children to rank them from the most general to the most particular, for example 'animals', 'four-legged', 'canine', 'dogs', 'wild/domestic', etc.
2 Ask children to create their own hierarchical concept maps. Give several lists and the option for children to choose which list they want to map.

Mapping stories
1 Choose a familiar story or extract from a story.
2 Help children prepare a list of concepts from the story.
3 Reorganise the list from the most important to the least important in the story.
4 Discuss the list and help them create a concept map from the story.

Mapping chosen topics
1 Ask children to prepare a concept map on any topic, for example a sport or hobby they know well.
2 Display/share their maps, encouraging positive comments.

Knowledge maps

Staring at a textbook is one of the most inefficient ways of learning facts. It is when we are actively processing the facts, doing something with them, that they are likely to stay in the memory. Creating a knowledge map is a technique that can work well when there are a lot of facts to learn, as in science, geography or history.

Here is one way of helping a young child or group of children to create a knowledge map:

1   Provide some plain cards, for example postcards, some coloured pens and reference materials such as a textbook, a reference book, lesson notes or a computer database.
2   Select 12 (or more) different facts on a topic of research, and write each one on a card using as few words as possible, and different colours for the words, drawings, numbers, etc.
3   Lay out the fact cards on a table or floor. Arrange them in any shape you wish, for example a tree, a circle, a line, a ladder, etc. so they make a connecting pattern.
4   Play a memory game. Turn all the cards over, except one. Ask children to test each other. Can they choose a card, and remember what it says? Check by turning over the card.
5   Display and discuss the knowledge map design, for example by gluing the cards onto a chart, or by keeping the cards loose in a file so that pupils can experiment with different map designs and can add more fact cards to the collection.

Graphic organisers

Children should be introduced to a variety of ways of organising information in graphic form (see Figure 5.3). Knowing different ways of mapping information will give them a means of processing any information for better understanding, and they will also be able to use their preferred way of making thinking maps. Research shows that there is no one way that is best or which suits all people. Some prefer a linear arrangement, some geometric forms, others more free-flowing organic structures. This has a lot to do with individual learning style preference, as well as the experience of the learner. Which ways of organising thinking have you tried? Which suit you best?

Graphic organisers and other visual tools can provide a good focus for collaborative learning. They can engage students in the shared processing of information and ideas, for example by using:

● cognitive mapping as a group activity to create a common frame of reference for thinking
● a cognitive map as a tangible outcome of group discussion.

Research shows that concept mapping will not only help students to remember more, and provide opportunities for 'higher order' processing of information, it also provides opportunities for shared and cooperative thinking that can be both stimulating and enjoyable.[7] The use of cognitive mapping can teach students how to shape, organise and communicate their thinking. As one child put it, 'I like seeing what I think, and I like seeing what others think.' Another added, 'It is easier to show what you think than to say what you think.' A third said, 'It gives you a chance to see what you think first and to think about it afterwards.' Wherever they want to go, or whatever they need to learn, knowing how to make a map could help them to find their way.

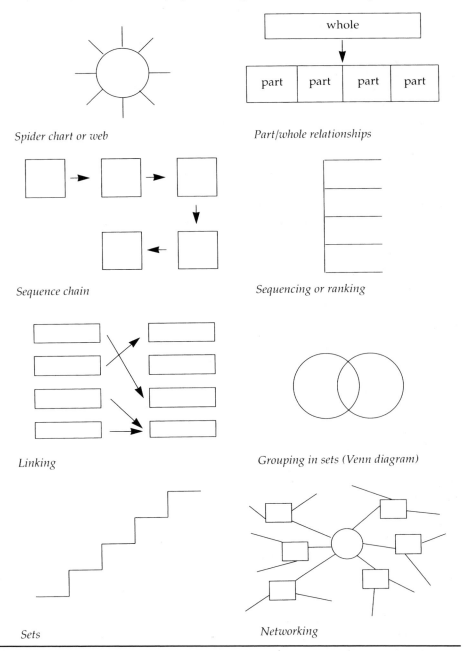

Figure 5.3 Think links – some visual tools for thinking

Summary

Visual tools can provide powerful aids to memory, understanding and concept development. Concepts are organising ideas that help us make sense of the world, and a child's learning is developed through organising information and ideas into patterns and frameworks of understanding. Graphic organisers and other cognitive mapping strategies help students to represent thinking in visual form, to depict relationships between facts and concepts, and relate new information to prior knowledge. Mapping can take many forms and be used to support a wide range of contexts for learning. Concept mapping can also provide a focus for group discussion and be a means to facilitate collaborative learning.

LIVERPOOL
JOHN MOORES UNIVERSITY

6 Creativity and learning

Creative thinking can help children make learning their own.

To him whose elastic and vigorous thought keeps pace with the sun, the day is perpetual morning.

Henry Thoreau

I learn best when I learn in my own way.

Crystal, aged 9

A class of young children was being taught about the importance of dental hygiene, and the risks of needing to have false teeth when they were older. One of the children responded: 'My grandma doesn't need false teeth.' 'Do you know why not?' asked the teacher. 'Yes', said the child, 'she's dead.'

We become creative when we are able to look at things from a new perspective. Einstein, who believed that the key to learning was flexible thinking, said:

> *To raise new questions, new problems, to regard old problems from a new angle requires creative imagination, and makes real advances.*

According to Piaget, 'To understand is to invent.'[1] We make knowledge our own 'by reconstructing it through some creative operation of the mind'. 'The mind once stretched by a new idea', said Oliver Wendell Holmes, 'never regains its original dimensions.'

Any learning that is not routine needs creativity. Unless the learner has complete knowledge of an area of learning, then creativity will be needed to help develop, adapt and apply understanding that is at present partial or incomplete. When knowledge is complete, we have no need to process it further, there is no need to think things through. To take account of new knowledge, develop new ideas or design solutions to new problems requires creative thinking. Creative, or divergent, thinking offers the chance to see more in any situation.

One of the reasons that creativity is needed in learning is that intelligence alone is not sufficient to realise learning potential. Intelligent people are not necessarily successful at thinking and learning. They may fall into what Edward de Bono calls the 'intelligence trap' of making instant judgements, of jumping to conclusions, without taking time to think about and explore alternatives. They may close off the opportunities to think and learn more. This impulsivity, or tendency to premature closure, is a characteristic of under-achieving children at all levels of intelligence. Thinking is defined by de Bono as 'the operating skill with which intelligence acts upon experience'. One of the characteristics of creative thinking is exploration, the ability to explore a situation before making a judgement. Creative thinking skills are not automatic, but they can be developed.[2]

LIVERPOOL
JOHN MOORES UNIVERSITY

I.M. MARSH LRC
Tel: 0151 231 5216

Creativity, intelligence and achievement

Creativity seems to be a capacity that is separate from intelligence, and the ways these combine can lead to very different learning styles and levels of achievement. Children scoring high on intelligence tests are not necessarily creative. When researchers compared samples of children having high and low scores on tests to measure intelligence and on tests to measure creativity covering educational, psychological and social dimensions, they summarised their findings as follows:[3]

- *High creativity + high intelligence*. These children can exercise within themselves both control and freedom, both adult-like and child-like kinds of behaviour.
- *High creativity + low intelligence*. These children are in angry conflict with themselves and with their school environment and are beset with feelings of unworthiness and inadequacy. In a stress-free context, they can blossom forth cognitively.
- *Low creativity + high intelligence*. These children can be described as 'addicted' to school achievement. Academic failure would be conceived by them as catastrophic, so that they must continually strive for academic excellence to avoid the possibility of pain.
- *Low creativity + low intelligence*. Basically bewildered, these children are engaged in various defensive social activities and regressions such as passivity or psychosomatic symptoms.

Research suggests that creativity can be an important element in the achievement of children whatever their intelligence or social background, and that creative thinking and doing can help develop the potential both of individuals and of human institutions such as schools or commercial organisations. But what is creativity? How do we assess it and develop it?

Across the world countries are reforming approaches to teaching and learning to better prepare young people for the complex and challenging demands of the future. The development of talent and creativity are being given a high priority in these reforms. Talent refers to the possession of a high degree of aptitude or skill in a given area (such as music or mathematics). Creativity is a more generic set of abilities applicable to a range of domains. But what are these creative abilities? Why are they important? How do we teach for creative learning?

What is creativity?

> *If I knew what creativity was, I'd know if I was creative.*
> Jane, aged 10

Creativity lies at the heart of what it means to be human. Creativity is not just about the arts or certain people. We all have the capacity for creative thinking – for generating and extending ideas, suggesting hypotheses, applying imagination and looking for alternative innovative outcomes.

The following are some characteristics of creative people. They:

- are flexible
- are curious
- connect ideas
- accept disorder
- are unorthodox
- show aesthetic taste
- enjoy experimenting
- are curious, inquisitive
- are open to new experience
- have the courage to take risks
- enjoy humour and playfulness
- see similarities and differences
- are independent and self-reliant
- are persistent and goal-directed
- question accepted ways of doing things.

These are all qualities that need to be fostered by teachers and caregivers, if children are to develop as creative learners.

Many attempts have been made to define creativity. The National Advisory Committee Report on Creative and Cultural Education offered the following definition for creativity. Creativity is 'imaginative activity fashioned so as to yield an outcome that is of value as well as original'.[4] Howard Gardner[5] described it as 'the ability to solve problems and fashion products and to raise new questions', and Bill Lucas[6] as 'a state of mind in which all our intelligences are working together'. Part of the reason for this diversity of definitions is that creativity can be seen as a property of people (who we are), processes (what we do) or products (what we make).

Creativity is about:

- people – self-esteem and confidence *who we are*
- processes – creative skills and knowledge *how we do things*
- products – creative outcomes *what* we do.

Creativity relates to the whole person – the hand, the heart and the head. It is about what we do, feel and think, when we do things of value that express who we are.

Creativity can be exercised in any lesson and through any activity. It is the buzz that comes from thinking, saying or doing things that are new or different. Bruner defines creativity as something that produces 'effective surprise', as when a teacher said to her class at the start of a lesson: 'I want you to surprise me' or at the end of the lesson: 'What surprised me was the way . . .'

Creativity remains hard to define. If we value creativity, we need to speak about it, to make it evident in our documents and to engage in discussing it with colleagues and pupils. In one school, children can identify when they have been creative, what they have done that is creative and can say what they understand by the term. The following are some definitions given by children:

Creativity is stretching further on knowledge, inventing ideas to help your thinking.
Chris, aged 10

Creative thinking is like thinking of all different objects or things in your own way.
Natasha, aged 10

Children have their own way of looking at the world. It is important, therefore, to find creative ways for them to express what they think and feel. The heart of creativity is self expression. 'There is so much inside me that doesn't come out', says Pat, a dyslexic child, aged eight. As one teacher put it, 'Creativity is about showing your way of looking at the world.' We need to find creative ways to help children express what they think and feel.

Creative thinking and activity can help children become more engaged with their learning, showing increased levels of motivation and self-esteem. Developing the capacity for creative thinking empowers children with the flexible skills they will need to face an uncertain future. Employers are seeking a workforce of creative people who are adaptable, innovative, can solve problems and communicate well with others. The capacity for creative thinking, speaking and listening will enable children to lead more successful lives. It will help develop those habits of mind that will enable them to solve problems in their own way. As Terry, aged 12, said, 'You need to try things in different ways so you find your own best way.'

There is no conflict between fostering creativity and improving academic achievement. Inspection evidence shows that the best teachers place a strong emphasis on creative and flexible teaching and on the creative development and achievements of their pupils. Creative teachers plan for multi-level learning. They have creative learning objectives, as well as curriculum objectives and targets. They link learning to real-life experiences and offer children the chance to make creative choices – they know this is important for learning and for life. As Tony, aged eight, put it:

I've got to learn to do it my way because that's what you have to do outside school, when there's no teacher or nothing to tell you.

Assessing creative thinking

The mind is an attention-focusing device. We become creative when we can vary and extend the focus of attention, when we are able to see and think of possibilities beyond the given information. We construct, we invent, we play with ideas. We have different capacities for creative thinking, and these capacities can be expanded and developed through practice. Typically this kind of divergent thinking comes in focused bursts, in response to a stimulus. But how good are we, or our children, at creative thinking?

Various tests have been designed to practise and to assess levels of creative thinking. The following are examples of three kinds of test:

- a drawing test, where students are asked to create a design from a simple given drawn shape or pattern
- a visualisation test, where students are asked of a given drawing 'What is it?' and try to list as many different possible items the drawing may be trying to represent
- a verbal test, where students are asked, for example, to generate creative ideas from a given verbal stimulus, for example 'How many uses can you think of for a . . . ?'

Drawing test

The following example is from the Torrance Tests of Creative Thinking (figural section):[7]

1 Give each student a page of A4 with a set of 20 circles arranged in orderly lines on each side of the page, making a total of 40 circles.
2 Invite them to draw as many interesting and unusual things involving the use of a circle as they can in 10 minutes. If necessary, give an example, for example a self-portrait. How many different things can they draw?
3 Ask them to put a caption under each drawing (optional).

Torrance suggests this test can be used to assess what he identifies as the four dimensions of creative thinking:

● *Fluency* – the number of different ideas generated. Assess this by counting the total number of different things drawn. (A drawing can use one or many circles.)
● *Flexibility* – the number of different categories of ideas. Count the number of different categories used, for example ball/football/other balls would be one category.
● *Originality* – the divergence of ideas from conventional or common choices. Score each drawing 0, 1 or 2 for originality. If everybody draws it, for example a face, score 0, if only a few draw it, for example a screw, score 1, if only one person draws it, for example a lamp base, score 2. The total score = originality rating.
● *Elaboration* – the detailed expression of ideas: assess the amount of detail given in each picture. This is very difficult to mark objectively.

Ask students to give themselves a score for fluency and flexibility, to identify their most original ideas and to compare across the group. Torrance found that high scores in originality and elaboration gave the highest correlation with creative ability. He also found some very individual creative responses did not score highly on these measures, for example a child who incorporated all the circles into a bee's honeycomb!

Visualisation test

Figure 6.1 is an example of a visualisation test, 'What is it?' Look at the shape and list as many things as you can think of that the shape might represent.

Figure 6.1 An example of a visualisation test

Suggestions from a group of children in response to this test included: sun, moon, star, light, torch, light, octopus, raindrop, well, spider's web, wheel, water splash, dandelion, volcano, explosion, firework, hair rising, button, bell, seed, bullet hole, bottle top, loudspeaker, moon crater, satellite, compass, eye, jet engine, ring, fountain, electricity, cog, water wheel, flower head, squashed spider, happiness, roads, headdress of the Statue of Liberty, legs sticking out from under a parasol, etc.

Verbal test

An example of a verbal test of divergent thinking is 'How many uses?' in which students are asked a question like 'How many alternative uses can you think of for . . . (a familiar object such as a blanket, barrel, brick, sock, paper clip, a shoebox, an elastic band, a human hair, toothbrush, compact disc, milk bottle, sock . . .)?

The tests described above can be conducted with students aged from eight to adulthood, but their use in identifying creative potential is highly debatable. Such tests can, however, provide a useful focus for exercising creativity, and for discussing creativity and the criteria used for judging it. In this kind of test there is no right answer, assessment is subjective and tests or retests often produce widely diverse scores. There is no test that can assess the potential for creativity of any individual. We all have creative potential and the capacity for self-expression.

Developing creative thinking

Torrance[8] suggests that creativity is:

a process of becoming sensitive to problems, deficiences, gaps in knowledge, missing elements, disharmonies, and so on; identifying the difficulty; searching for solutions, making guesses, or formulating hypotheses about the deficiencies, testing and retesting these hypotheses and possibly modifying and retesting them; and finally communicating the results.

Creativity is a form of intelligence that can be trained and developed like any other mode of thinking. It is not merely a question of playing with things, of randomness or chance, but at its best has to do with serious and sustained effort in thinking about any area of learning.

In the UK, Edward de Bono's work is perhaps the most well-known in the area of creativity The three main de Bono creative thinking programmes are 'lateral thinking', CoRT and 'six thinking hats'.[9] These consist of a number of 'tools' applicable to a wide range of teaching situations. The tools are simple but powerful strategies for getting people to think more widely, to promote deeper reflection, and to avoid impulsivity. One of the most useful CoRT 'Thinking Tools' is PMI (Plus, Minus, Interesting points).

PMI: Plus, Minus, Interesting points

'Think before you leap' says de Bono, and PMI is a strategy that aims to force thinking about any situation before coming to a judgement about it. The process involves listing all the good points, bad points and interesting points about a given idea, object or event.

- 'Plus' relates to the positive elements of the topic.
- 'Minus' relates to the negative elements.

- 'Interesting' relates to those points that are neither good nor bad, but are regarded as neutral observations, comments or points of interest.

PMI is one of the most useful and effective tools for directing attention and generating thinking about different aspects of a topic, situation or piece of work.

- I'm not sure about this. Let's do a PMI.
- To find out more about what we think, let's do a PMI.
- There are two options. Let's do a PMI on each.

Pictures, objects or texts can be subjected to creative analysis using the PMI method. The following are examples of activities with which to practise divergent thinking using PMI.

TASK 25

Assessing – positive, negative and interesting points

Make a list for each category of good points under 'Plus', bad points under 'Minus', and 'Interesting' points about a given topic, for example:

1 Attendance at school should not be compulsory for any child.
2 People should wear badges to show if they are in a good or bad mood that day.
3 All seats should be taken out of buses.
4 Think about what you have done today, yesterday or during the last week. What were the positive, negative and interesting points in your life during this time?
5 Choose a book, picture or TV film and do a PMI on it.

Six thinking hats

The 'six thinking hats' reflect de Bono's analysis of the various cognitive processes involved in being creative. They encourage people to think about any topic or issue in divergent and creative ways. Each hat is a different colour and represents a different way of thinking.

The colours of the six hats can be summarised as follows:

- white – neutral and objective, concerned with facts and figures
- red – emotions and feeling
- black – negative and looks for problems, risks and dangers
- yellow – positive and looks for benefits
- green – innovative and creative
- blue – control of the thinking process and of the other hats.

Creative thinking is about generating ideas and increasing the breadth of perception. Instead of a narrow focus, we try to review the whole field. The 'thinking hats' is a tool that aims to expand the focus of attention. What factors should we consider in this situation? If we want children to have the ability to take in many things, things that are within the situation and things outside relevant to the situation, things now present and things that may happen in the future, children will need to have experience in broadening their perception, to look beyond the given, and to consider all factors.

Research with junior-age children shows that the different thinking hats are quickly forgotten if used only once. But if repeated in a variety of learning contexts over a period of time they can become a 'thinking frame' that is remembered and used.

The following tasks provide practice in the use of the 'thinking hats' technique.

TASK 26

Thinking hats

Discuss in a group using different 'hats' all the different factors involved in the following for each of the following:

1 Your family have decided to move to a new home. What factors should they take into account in deciding on a new home?
2 You are choosing a summer holiday. What factors should you keep in mind?
3 What factors make for a good teacher?
4 What makes for a good story? List all the factors that might be included in writing a good story.
5 You are designing a chair. What factors should you take into account?

Other points of view

At the heart of moral, social and cultural education and of all learning relating to other people are acts of imagination. We develop empathy and understanding of others when our perception is broadened and we have the ability to see other points of view. 'The hardest thing', says Jody, aged 10 'is to think what it would really be like to be someone else.'

One way to broaden perception is to try to see things from another person's point of view. For the child, and perhaps for us all, this is a difficult challenge. It requires an ability to listen to the views expressed by other people, and to make an imaginative leap to understand their feelings and ideas. This leap of imagination is fundamental to moral development and to an understanding of others (or what has been called *interpersonal intelligence*).

An obvious way into thinking about other points of view is to consider both sides of an argument or conflict. It can be fruitful when stopping a quarrel or fight between two children to get each to state their own point of view without the other interrupting. Stories and drama also provide good opportunities to look at different points of view:

- Does everyone think the same thing?
- What do you think? What does he/she think?
- What do the others think?
- What are they feeling? Why?
- What do you think is going through his/her/their mind?

The following are some tasks that aim to encourage seeing things from another's point of view.

TASK 27

Empathy – recognising other points of view

List what you think the views are of different people in these examples.

1 A father and mother forbid their son and daughter to stay up past 10 o'clock to watch a TV programme they want to see. What are the different views of the parents and the children?

2 Someone wants to sell you a second-hand bicycle. What are their views and your views?

3 You lend a friend some money to buy a lottery ticket. Your friend wins a prize with the ticket. Who does the prize belong to? What might be the different points of view of you and your friend?

4 A burglar breaks into your house and steals everything of value that can be found. Your parents call the police, who say they will try their best to catch the thief. What are the views of your parents, the burglar and the police?

5 Choose a book, picture or video programme and list the different thoughts, feelings and points of view of the characters.

Empathy, like all forms of creative thinking can be learned and developed. All courses of study should allow for some use of creative thinking. All forms of learning should allow for some divergent thinking (called by de Bono *lateral thinking*). 'You cannot dig a hole in a different place', says de Bono, 'by digging the same hole deeper.' Trying harder with the same ideas and same approach may not solve the problem. This is especially so with those having trouble with learning. They may need to move 'laterally' to try new ideas and a new approach. Lateral thinking includes a number of methods for escaping from established ideas in order to find new ones.

Provocation

Children should be given the chance to think in new ways – but how? One way is through provocation, what creative thinking guru Roger von Oech[10] calls 'a whack on the side of the head'. He argues that we need to be whacked out of habitual thought patterns and provoked to look at what you are doing in a new way. (The word 'po' has been coined by de Bono to describe a similar kind of 'provocative operation'.) One technique is 'provocation in role', which entails the teacher or other 'agent provocateur' playing the devil's advocate in discussion with children by challenging all or any received moral and scientific assumptions with a view to building up a child's confidence and resilience in argument. A provocative statement is any that will stimulate creative thought, response or discussion.

Examples of provocative statements might include:

● There is no point in going to school.
● Nothing is true.
● I can do whatever I want.
● A triangle can have four sides.
● Adults know more than children so what they say is never wrong.

What provocative statements can you create to get your children thinking and responding?

What if . . . ?

You see things and say 'Why?' But I dream things and say 'Why not?'
G.B. Shaw

- What if animals could speak?
- What if plants could walk?
- What if we could live forever?
- What if the earth stopped revolving and the sun did not rise?
- What if you were allowed to run the school?

'What ifs' provide a wishful-thinking kind of provocation by adding some impossible feature or picking out some feature of an item and imagine it was missing. For example:

- What essential features of the following could you imagine leaving out of a house/school/bicycle/library/birthday? (For example, 'What if your house had no . . . ?')
- What features could you imagine adding to school/parents/clothes/sleep/sports? (For example, 'Wouldn't it be nice if . . .')

Can you or your children create 10 'What if . . .' impossibilities. Choose, draw and discuss your most interesting idea.

Synectics – making the familiar strange

An important element in creative problem-solving is making the familiar strange – looking at the same problem in different ways. Synectics research identified three methods of creating metaphor for helping to see the familiar in new ways:[11]

- *Direct analogy* – making a simple comparison, for example: 'How is a teacher like a tuna sandwich?'
- *Personal analogy* – imagining being the thing, for example, 'A candle is not alive, but it looks alive when it burns. How would you feel if you were a candle burning in a camping tent?'
- *Symbolic analogy* – creating a compressed conflict (oxymoron), for example, 'What is an example of a careful collision?'

Carl Sandburg, the American poet, once said: 'Poetry is the synthesis of hyacinths and biscuits.' Here he was taking two unrelated words or images and putting them together to make the familiar strange. One way of doing this is to take two unrelated words or ideas and try to join them with a linking thought. If what we think about one thing is also true of another we are reasoning by analogy. Children can be encouraged to create an analogy by asking questions such as 'What is similar to this object?', 'How are they similar?', 'What do you know about one object that might be true of the other?'

The following are examples of students creating metaphors about themselves:

- I am undiscovered gold lying in the hills, waiting to be found.
- I am like a grape, just one of a bunch, but I am full of juicy goodness.
- I am like a pawn in a game of chess, but without me the game would not work.

TASK 28

Creating metaphors

Think of as many answers as you can for these questions. There are no right or wrong answers:

1 a) What answers can you find for these riddles?
- Why is summer like a bridge?
- Which animal is like a rubber band?
- Which colour is quickest?

   b) Create more metaphorical riddles of your own by linking two seemingly unrelated ideas.

2 a) Make up some metaphors (or analogies) about yourself.
- What kind of food are you?
- What kind of furniture are you?
- What kind of animal are you?

   b) Think of some more categories, and make up some more metaphors.

3 Create some more metaphors about yourself:
- What is your mind/brain like?
- What is your life like?

Creative thinking programmes aim to provide a systematic approach to creative learning. Some people find creative problems both challenging and fun, but others may not be so keen. The key question is: can pupils apply what they learn from working on abstract problems to real-life learning situations? Evidence suggests that many children are not very good at this, so teachers need to look for ways to develop creativity across the curriculum.

Creativity across the curriculum

What promotes creativity is a questioning classroom, where:

- teachers and pupils ask unusual and challenging questions
- new connections are made
- ideas are represented in different ways, visually, physically and verbally
- there are fresh approaches to problems
- the effects of ideas and actions are assessed in ways that support learning.

There are blocks to creativity such as 'defensive teaching', where children are asked to work for long periods with low demand and little active input, where outcomes are controlled and prescribed, and tasks too repetitive. Creativity occurs where there is time to explore, experiment and play with ideas, for example through ICT or with a range of creative partners. 'I like working with others', says Claire, 'because sometimes you don't know what you think until you hear what they say.'

Creative thinking focuses on 'knowing how' as well as 'knowing what'. The National Curriculum (2000) recognises creative thinking as one of the key skills in thinking and in learning to learn. These skills are embedded in all subjects and enable pupils to:

- generate and extend ideas
- suggest hypotheses
- apply imagination
- consider things from alternative viewpoints
- look for alternative outcomes.

Creative teachers try to build opportunities for creativity into every lesson. They share creative teaching ideas, such as creative lesson starters. In one school, as the children enter the class they are greeted with classical music and a thinking challenge, which might be a verbal, mathematical or visual puzzle, a problem, investigation or challenge such as working out the similarities and differences between ketchup and blood. They tackle the daily task in their A4 size 'Thinking Books', which is then shared in class but not marked. Children find these 'thinking starters' to the day a good preparation for the lessons ahead. As pupil Georgie put it, 'I think I am most creative in the morning because when I think deeply it gets my mind working for the rest of the day.'[12]

Creative teachers look for evidence of pupils applying their imagination; generating their own questions, hypotheses, ideas and outcomes; developing skills through creative activity and using judgement to assess their own or others' creative work. They reward those children who are creative risk takers. In one school, time for creativity is built into each day. For example each afternoon begins with an 'artistic performance', in which children are invited to share something they have created, such as music, a play, a song, a dance, a poem, a story, an improvisational game, magic or even juggling. The teacher seeks to provide children with opportunities for creative expression ('a time to shine') that might otherwise not fit into a busy curriculum.

Creativity is about individual choice and self-expression. From the early years, there needs to be a focus on developing independence and self-direction in learning. Creative learners need creative contexts for learning and to be given as much creative autonomy as possible. For example, in one school all 6 year olds are given their own 'Inventions Book' in which to design creative solutions to everyday problems. For older children, a creative project on 'shoes' was the context for learning about materials, and for designing a dazzling array of individual shoe creations.

The following are some creative teaching strategies that can be applied to a wide range of curriculum areas.

Use imagination

Think of new ideas, speculate on what might be possible and apply imagination to improve outcomes.

Question cues:
- What might happen if . . . (if not)?
- Design a new way to . . .
- Suggest an improvement on . . .

Generate more ideas

Generate many responses, encourage thinking of alternatives and greater fluency of ideas.

Question cues:

- How many kinds of . . . can you think of?
- List all . . . that could be used for . . .
- What might be the arguments for . . . (and against . . .)?

Experiment with alternatives

Be willing to change one's initial ideas, see things another way, experiment with alternative approaches.

Question cues:

- How else might you . . . ?
- Think of five ways of/questions to ask about/reasons for . . .
- List ten things you could do with . . . (a shape, recipe, piece of music, picture, object, design brief, photo, news story, etc.)

Be original

Think of novel ideas, unique solutions, and design original plans.

Question cues:

- Design a game for . . .
- Invent a way to . . .
- Think of a way to improve . . . (an object, game, text, plan, etc.)

Expand on what we do and know

Elaborate on what you know, build on a given situation, make it more interesting.

Question cues:

- What might we add . . . (for example, to a story, a picture, a design)?
- What might we change . . . (for example, to make it different, more interesting)?
- What is another way to . . . (for example, solve problem, apply algorithm, investigate hypothesis)?

Exercise creative judgement

Assess what we have thought/done, evaluate the process and judge the outcome.

Question cues:

- What criteria should we use to judge whether . . . ?
- What is good/could be improved/is interesting about . . . ?
- What could/should you/we do next . . . ?

The exercise of judgement is about considering:

- Choices – were the right choices made?
- Alternative outcomes – is it better or worse than . . . ?
- Possibilities – could/should it be different, and if so how?

Creativity is about choices, alternatives, and possibilities

The world is full of alternatives, possibilities and choices. But we don't always see them. This is especially true of the learning child, who often comes to believe there is only one answer, only one right way to do things. We need to be alert to alternatives, to possible new directions, and to have the courage to sometimes choose 'the road less travelled by'. We talk of being 'blinkered', and of 'tunnel vision'. As learners we talk of 'getting stuck', and of not knowing what to do, where to turn, which way to go. If children value the practice of seeking alternatives, they will be better placed to generate options when they need them.

There are many sorts of alternatives:

- *viewpoints* – looking at the same thing in different ways, from different viewpoints
- *actions* – seeing alternative possible courses of action in a given situation
- *solutions* – being aware of alternative solutions to a problem
- *ways of working* – realising that there are different ways of tackling a problem
- *explanations* – suggesting alternative explanations and hypotheses to explain how something happened
- *plans* – devising alternative plans for approaching a task
- *designs* – creating alternative designs for meeting a need or purpose.

Encourage children to look for alternatives, to be alert to the multiplicity of possibilities. Support the belief that they always have a choice. If one way does not work, look for alternatives. If there seems to be only one way, look for alternatives. You may not find them, but your approach is intelligent. As one child commented, 'There is always a different way, even if you can't find it.'

TASK 29
Seeking alternatives
Make a list of options, alternatives and possibilities to help in making a decision about the following problems or situations.
1 You discover your best friend is a thief. What alternatives do you have?
2 As you walk along the street, you see a woman collapse to the ground. Why could this have happened? What could you do?
3 A car is found crashed in a ditch. There is no driver. What happened?
4 Some places are dirty because people drop litter and cans everywhere. What could you do to solve this problem?
5 You and your friends decide to raise money for charity. Which charity? What could you do?

The most difficult thing to do is to look for alternatives when you don't have to. We tend to do things out of habit, to work mindlessly. What can help us to be more flexible in our thinking, and more alert to possibilities? Questions to ask include:

- Is there another way?
- Can we come up with an alternative suggestion?

- Is there a possibility we have not thought of?
- What other choices have we got?
- Have we considered all the options?

When we begin to look for alternatives, we should be clear about the purpose of the alternative. Task 29 provides sample ways to encourage looking for alternatives:

The following are some ideas for activities that can help develop creative thinking.[13]

Link-ups

Choose any word. Write it down. Look at it and write the first word that comes into your head that is somehow associated with it. Continue to add words, building up a sequence of associations. See how long you can keep the chain going. Or say the words aloud while your partner scribes them. A more challenging version is to try to reach, in a chain of association, a very different word from the first word.

Picture this

Choose a reproduction of a painting.

- Write any words that come into your mind when you look at the picture.
- Try weaving a story around the image.
- Describe the picture without showing it to your partner. Can they visualise it?
- Visualise a picture that they describe, and draw it from their description.

Picture construction

Scatter dots over a page. Make several copies. Create pictures using the dots as starting points.

Story ending

Any problem can have several solutions, so any story can have more than one ending.

- Read a short story, stop halfway through, and complete the story yourself. How many endings can you devise? Which is best? Why?
- This is reputed to be the shortest science fiction story in the world:

After the nuclear war, earth was dead; nothing grew, nothing lived. The last man sat alone in a room. There was a knock on the door . . .

Can you complete the story?

Poetry pieces

From an anthology or poetry book, write lines or fragments from different poems on slips of paper (a pair or group can combine their efforts). Select at random some slips of paper. Read the fragments of poetry. Try to visualise what they are about. Try to compose a poem (or piece of prose) using one or more of the pieces of poetry and your own words.

Hear this

Shut your eyes while you listen to a new piece of music. What picture(s) come into your mind? What words come into your mind? What title would you give the music? What does it make you feel or think?

Sentence making

Choose four or five different initial letters, for example W, C, E, N. How many sentences can you generate using these four letters? Example: 'We can eat nuts.' Or five letters, for example E, G, B, D, F? This is a test of verbal fluency.

Common problems

What problems might arise, for example in taking a bath, getting up in the morning, cooking a meal, going to school/work, watching TV, playing with friends, buying shoes, etc? Share problems, suggest solutions.

Improvements

How could you improve, for example a door, a desk, the human body, school, law and order, etc?

Create a character

Choose a person you would like to be. What is your name? What do you look like? Where do you live? What do you do? What are your likes/dislikes? What is your story?

Computers and creativity

Computers can stifle creativity if they simply provide ready-made answers and children are passive consumers rather than active investigators of their own learning. As Picasso once said, 'Computers are useless. They only give us answers.' However there are a number of ways in which creativity may be stimulated through information and communication technology (ICT). Given the important role computers have in the lives of learners and teachers, developing ways to use them as creative tools is a vital challenge.[14]

Computers offer possibilities for children to develop their creativity through being presented with problems and investigations involving diverse and uncertain outcomes.

Many computer *games* involve opportunities for creativity through:

- differentiated levels of challenge and personal response
- open-ended investigations which exercise 'what if . . .' thinking
- providing a stimulus for imagination.

Even though the worlds that they can explore in computer games are in fact predetermined by the program, they are often complex, with events, characters, problems to be solved, and some kind of 'quest' to achieve.

The creative benefits are enhanced through discussion with others, and responding to such questions as: 'What kind of world is this?', 'What options were there?', 'What else might you have done?' The creativity of computers is enhanced through dialogue with people, when children are no longer glued to the screen but are sharing their thoughts and ideas with others.

Computers provide a technology for fostering relationships in new ways, transcending geographical, cultural, age and expertise boundaries, as *e-mail* and *web-based communications* demonstrate. Technology provides a potential for the fostering of creative partnerships, within and outside of school.

Another way in which computers can engage with individual creativity is their *ability to present and manipulate information* in a wide variety of ways, which can challenge each child's cognitive abilities. By using this facility for sound, colour and movement, cartoon-like animation, displaying information in the form of graphs and charts, or in the form of 3-D models, children whose dominant learning styles need information in visual, auditory or modelled form, are much better provided for.

Another creative capability which computers can help develop is the use of *control technology through robots and programs* such as LOGO. Children can create the instructions which control the movement of a computerised machine such as a turtle or robot. In this way computers become 'tools to think with'.[15]

Computers also offer a tool for *creating works of art*. Painting, drawing and design programmes provide opportunities for creating a virtual environment for investigating and trying possibilities in ways which are not possible using the tactile materials. Computers also offer the facility for writing music on to a score, and playing with sound effects. Music can be composed via a range of programs allowing children to 'play' with harmony and sound effects in ways not dreamt of by Beethoven or Bernstein.

Electronic whiteboards offer further opportunities for teachers to be creative in their lesson presentation and for pupils 'minds to be stretched' by a whole world of resources. Class discussion can be enhanced by a web page or video clip made immediately visible to all. There is great scope here for generating 'effective surprise' and the creative engagement of children.

Computers can become a 'democratic' space, open to all, in which pupils and teachers can engage in both problem-finding and problem-solving. Creative use of ICT may also foster attitudes characteristic of life-long, high-level, creative achievement, such as:

- self-control
- sustained hard work
- determination and perseverance
- ability to take initiatives and to find relevant information
- ability to try new ideas and experiment with different approaches to a problem
- confidence to take risks in the face of uncertainty.

If the use of computers allows time for slower thinking (without undue time pressure), independent thinking (without the pressures of over-supervision) and time for experiment (choosing your own ways of working), its potential for creativity seems high.

The creative teacher

TASK 30

Questions on creativity and learning

These questions on creativity and learning are for reflection and discussion.

1 What are my/our views on creativity? What does 'creativity' mean?
2 How important is creativity? How important is it in my classroom?
3 How do I foster creativity? What opportunities do I provide?
4 What is the evidence of my pupils' creativity? What does their creativity look like?
5 Am I creative in my own teaching? What would help me be more creative?
6 Do my assessments support creative learning? Are my pupils engaged in assessing to learn?
7 How do I maintain my own creativity? How do I develop it?

Creative teachers celebrate diversity and doing things differently. They are passionate about pupils' learning and creativity. But they need time for reflection and dialogue about creativity and learning. They know that creativity is not just what is written into plans and documents but that it is given life through discussion and experiment.

Summary

Children can be helped to gain more from any learning situation if self-expression and creativity are encouraged. One of the defining characteristics of creativity is the ability to generate and explore alternatives. In practice, this means encouraging a divergent range of responses, to allow for individual patterns and styles of learning. Creativity is not directly related to intelligence, but is a separate set of skills – including visual and verbal skills – that can be developed and, to some extent, assessed. A number of creative thinking techniques and teaching strategies can be helpful in developing creative learning. Creativity needs to be developed across the curriculum and through use of ICT. Creative teachers need time to reflect on and develop their own creativity.

---

7 Collaborative learning

Co-operative group work develops social and cognitive aspects of learning.

What a child can do in co-operation today, he will be able to do alone tomorrow.
Vygotsky (1962)

I used to hate working with other people. Now I've worked in groups, I only hate working with some *other people.*
Kim, aged 8

Wayne was struggling with his reading. A rather quiet and withdrawn 8 year old, he was finding it very difficult to progress beyond the most basic of his reading scheme books. He was the least able reader in his class and his teacher was worried. A new idea had been tried in a local school. It was called *peer tutoring*, which meant that children worked in a structured way with a more able partner. So Wayne was paired with an older fluent reader – and they read together for 15 minutes a day for a term. 'At first', said his teacher, 'there didn't seem to be much progress, but by the end of the term Wayne had really taken off.' And he put it down, not to his teacher, but to his 'reading friend'. Wayne had learnt about reading and also something of the value of co-operative learning.

Every child is different. Even asking a simple question like 'What are clouds made of?' will elicit a range of responses from a group of children. All children have their own store of knowledge, ideas and experiences which they use to make sense of the world. Each child has unique abilities and a learning style all their own. Should the child then be best viewed as an individual learner, as an 'active scientist' exploring the world and developing increasingly complex structures of individual thought? If all learners are individuals, should all learning be individualised learning?

In the 1960s, there was a big movement towards individualised learning. It was called *programmed learning* and had a simple rationale: every child is individual and each has different needs, so each needs an individual programme to work through. Machines were devised and boxes of work cards and work books produced to allow each child to interact with the programme in his or her own way. Some good programmes were written, and they produced efficient learning outcomes. But these programmes became less effective with continued use if they were not mediated by a teacher. Many of the materials simply invited 'busyness', for example completing blanks in given sentences. The work was often repetitive and superficial, with little evidence of learning or thinking. The decisive influence on the success of such programmes was not the machine or the materials but the mediating influence of another human being. Learning can be an unassisted activity. A child is given a load of bricks, a student presented with a problem, an adult given a recipe or set of instructions, and they can respond to and relish an individual learning situation. But most learning takes place in a social context. As Bruner says: 'Making sense is a social process.'[1]

For Vygotsky, social interaction has a central role in a child's education.[2] It is through being with 'knowledgeable others' that a child's potential for learning is revealed. These knowledgeable others can be anybody – parents, siblings, friends, peers, teachers or other adults. Parents are usually the primary caretakers, but anyone can act as a caretaker of a child's learning. For example, some companies, like Anglo American, are offering company volunteers as 'reading partners' for children on weekly visits to school.

Much of our learning is founded on co-operatively achieved success. With others we can do more and achieve more than we can do on our own. The reason why human beings are, at present, the most successful of the animal species is that we are able to combine the flexibility and experimental brilliance of individuals, with the generative power of co-operative effort. Children learn best when they have access to the generative power of those around them. As one child said: 'I like working with others, they help you see what you are thinking.'

The basis of success-through-others is language and communication. It is through effective communication – 'co-operative talking' – that great institutions, social organisations and small task groups achieve success. We need to look therefore at two closely linked areas:

- *co-operative talking* – organising experience into thought with others
- *collaborative learning* – learning with others, in pairs, in small and in large groups.

The best conditions for learning exist when children have a challenge that extends their cognitive range. We help most when we encourage the child's reach to exceed its grasp. Too great a challenge risks ending in failure and frustration. Too little challenge and a child's potential will never be realised. For Vygotsky this potential – what he calls the *zone of proximal development* – exists not just in the child's mind. It lies as much in the 'social plane', in the skills, ideas and experiences of the social context in which she and her peers inhabit, as in the 'psychological plane' or internal functions of the mind. On this view, the role of the teacher is to provide the social and cognitive framework for learning, so that attention is drawn to the cognitive challenge of the task, and support is made available to meet that challenge.

Collaboration can provide social and cognitive support for learning. Co-operative group work involves children working together in pairs or small groups on a problem, investigation or another learning task that requires collaboration. Working together provides a context that can develop both their learning and social skills. As Marlene, aged 10 said, when asked why it was good to work with others, 'More heads are better than one head if you've got to get your head around something.'

Collaborative group work gives children the opportunity to:

- learn from each other
- engage in exploratory talk to deepen or broaden their understanding
- develop problem-solving skills and strategies
- learn to take turns, negotiate with others, see other points of view and argue their own point of view
- build relationships with a wider circle of people.

Another justification of collaborative work is that we are able to expect more from children who are working together than when working on their own. For collaborative groups to be successful, they have to be planned, monitored and supported. Teachers and caregivers need to help children recognise the importance of working together and to understand how it benefits their learning and social skills. Effective group work is more likely to happen when everyone understands the purpose, task and contribution expected from each individual involved. Children need clear success criteria for each activity agreed at the start of the session so they know what the teacher's expectations are. As Peter, aged nine, commenting on the criteria for success of his group, said:

> *We need to know before we start what we are meant to be doing and we need to keep reminding {people} because when you are with others it is easy to forget and to rely on them.*

We can learn more when working with others. But what form should this collaboration take?

Learning in pairs

> *Make your friends your teachers and mingle the pleasures of conversation with the advantages of instruction.*
> Gracian (1647)

Like many good ideas in education, children helping children is not new. The benefits of peer tutoring were known to the Greeks and Romans. As Comenius observed: 'Qui docet, discit' (Who teaches, learns). As teachers discover, there is no better way to learn something well than to teach it, and to teach something is often to learn it twice. It is a process that can benefit:

- *the tutor* – the helping child
- *the tutee* – the child who is helped
- *the teacher* – the mediator of the learning.

Goodlad[3] says that peer tutoring is 'humanly rewarding'. What are these rewards? Social benefits arise from creating a co-operative learning environment, in promoting a sense of common purpose and in social bonding. Gains in learning can include progress in subject areas, and in learning how to learn (metacognitive development).

The helping child (tutor) can benefit from taking on a nurturing role. Although they are teaching material they may have mastered, tutors can gain intellectual benefits in different ways. Putting their skills and knowledge to some purpose will help to consolidate their knowledge, fill in gaps, find new meanings and extend their conceptual frameworks. It also helps the child to understand more about the learning process, the possible blocks to learning and how to overcome them. As one child tutor put it:

> *Teaching someone is not easy. You have to remember a lot of what you've forgotten. It helps you understand what you went through at that age. Having a teacher is all right but having a friend too is better.*

For the child helped by another, the benefits can be considerable. The tutee is given some extra individual attention, with regular and responsive feedback on his or her efforts. The verbal interaction with a friend is of a personal and powerful kind, if it works well. The quality of teaching by a peer tutor will rarely match that of a trained teacher. Why is this so? Good teaching involves giving help when the learner faces difficulty, but offering less help when the learner shows signs of competence. Child tutors are ready to offer help, but tend not to pull back when the learner shows signs of success. Child tutors give specific concrete suggestions, and are less likely than adults to ensure the learner understands the connections between activities. Children are not as good as adults at 'scaffolding' the learning process for others.[4] They do not have the metacognitive skills of adults; they know less about the process of learning. But what they do offer is a direct help in learning, and help of a companionable kind. The tutor child can provide a model of learning, and demonstrate the required behaviour, such as reading or problem-solving in maths. The tutor can model how to learn as well as offer emotional support. As one child in a tutoring scheme remarked, 'It's like having an extra friend in the classroom.'

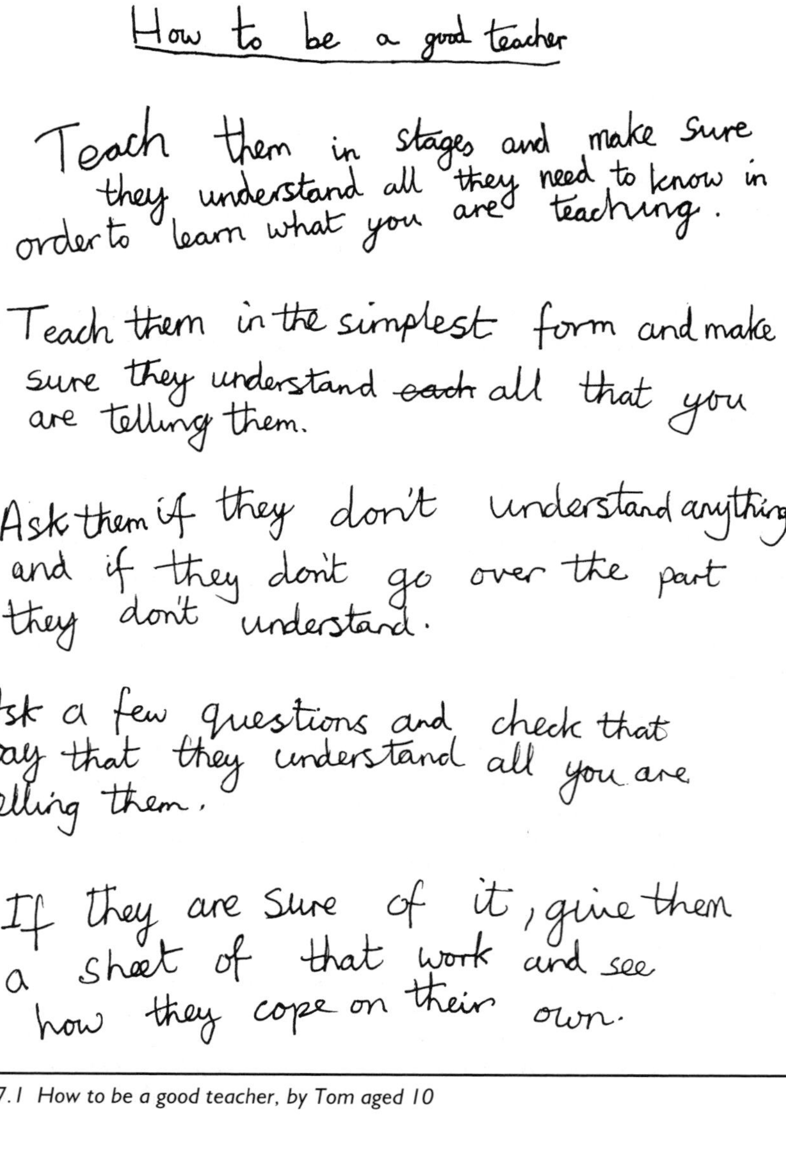

How to be a good teacher

Teach them in stages and make sure they understand all they need to know in order to learn what you are teaching.

Teach them in the simplest form and make sure they understand ~~each~~ all that you are telling them.

Ask them if they don't understand anything and if they don't go over the part they don't understand.

Ask a few questions and check that way that they understand all you are telling them.

If they are sure of it, give them a sheet of that work and see how they cope on their own.

Figure 7.1 How to be a good teacher, by Tom aged 10

What do teachers get out of it? Peer tutoring can free teachers from some of the routine work inherent in monitoring a whole class. To foster an 'apprenticeship' approach to learning, teachers will need to support both tutor and tutee, to ensure that a positive social relationship is being developed. As one teacher, after having set up a peer tutoring scheme reported, 'When it works we all benefit.'

Paired reading

I like reading with someone because it helps me to read by myself later.
    Jane, aged 8

There has been much research[5] into the benefits of paired reading. Originally intended for use with non-professional adults to help children with a reading disability, it has been found to have beneficial effects when used with non-readers, retarded readers, average and able readers. The recommended approach can be summed up as follows:

1 The tutee selects a book of interest.
2 The tutoring child, or teacher, checks that the book is within the tutee's competence, for example, by using the 'five finger test' (This is a simple readability check. Open the book at random, spread five fingers across the page. If the tutee can read the five words the fingers are pointing at, the book is probably appropriate. If there is difficulty in reading more than one word, then the book is probably too hard. If there is a problem with one word, then try again on another page.)
3 Tutor and tutee sit physically close.
4 Tutor and tutee talk about the book, before the tutee reads aloud, or they read the text together.
5 If the reader is stuck on a word, the tutoring child allows a pause (so the tutee can think and try guessing from the context or the initial sound of the word). The tutor then prompts (by giving a clue, such as the initial sound of the word).
6 Praise is a key feature of the method – praise for the child who is helped, and for the helper.

The process is simple. As Goodlad put it, all you need to decide is 'who is to teach what to whom and for what purpose, how and where, when and how often'.[6] Success in this kind of learning is made up of many small steps. The recipe is – keep it short, simple and sustained. The tutoring child (or adult) needs training, for example in the pause–prompt–praise method, and the process needs to be monitored so that there is a good 'match' and positive feelings between the partners.

Paired writing

For any writer, having a 'response friend' to share the first draft of a piece of writing can be useful in providing an audience for the work, as well as in proofreading for errors and improvements in style. But children need guidance, both on how to be a good writer and how to be a good response friend. Children find it helpful to have this information made explicit. As one 9 year old said, 'You can't make it better until you know how.' This know-how needs to be put into words, for it is not self-evident. Figure 7.2 shows the advice one teacher posted in her classroom about being a good writer and on being a good response friend.

Being a good writer

1 Draft your writing.
2 Read it aloud to yourself.
3 Think ... Do you want to add or change anything?
4 Read or show your writing to someone. Is there a good beginning and end?
5 Listen to what they say. Is there a way of making it better?
6 Can you make it even better?

Being a good 'response friend'

1 Read your friend's work, or listen carefully as your friend reads it.
2 Tell your friend at least two good things you liked about the wriring.
3 Think how they might improve their writing. Is there anything missing?
4 Can you help your friend make it better?

Figure 7.2 Being a good writer and a good 'response friend'

In learning how to learn, children need opportunities to teach, and opportunities to learn from each other. They can benefit from learning to learn in three different kinds of partnership:

- equal partners in terms of age and ability as response partners to share thinking work and problem-solving.
- tutor partners who are more able, such as older students or adults who can act as 'expert' helpers
- tutee partners who are less able can be tutored in specific learning tasks, giving them experience of being in the 'expert' tutoring mode.

Think–pair–share

One collaborative learning strategy found useful in all kinds of learning situations is summed up in the slogan: 'think–pair–share'. Often teachers use a 'one-response' strategy, meaning that one child responds in the class at a time. Think–pair–share is a multi-response strategy, applicable to all ages and abilities.

The stages of think–pair–share are:

1 Students *listen* while the teacher or another poses the question or problem.
2 Students are given time to *think* of a response.
3 Students then pair with a neighbour to *discuss* their response.
4 Finally students *share* their responses with the whole group.

The following are some activities that can encourage paired learning:

- *paired drawing* – one partner draws a picture, and describes the hidden picture to the other who tries to draw it from the description
- *mirror movement* – one child creates a sequence of bodily movements for the partner to try to follow at the same time

- *shared reading* – partners prepare a text, for example a news item, a story or a poem, for reading aloud between them to others
- *cartoons* – partners brainstorm ideas, one child draws, the other supplies captions
- *instructions* – partners work out instructions, rules and strategies for doing something, for example playing a game or making a model, then show others
- *paired stories* – partners create a story together to retell to others
- *paired assessment* – partners report on each other's work, picking out at least two good things about it and one thing to improve.

TASK 31

Peer tutoring

Think of a child who needs help in some aspect of learning.

1 Who could be a learning partner for that child?
2 What advice will the learning partner need?
3 Where should they meet? When, and how often?
4 In what ways can you support the partnership?

Working with partners should also give a child confidence to work in bigger groups.

Learning in a group

I like working in a group when you know what you have to do . . . when you each have a job. Otherwise you might just as well be on your own.

James, aged 8

If all teaching were done on an individual basis, a teacher could only spend a little amount of time with each individual. More time can be spent with children when they are grouped together, and they can learn more from working with each other.

The advantages of working in a group can include the development of:

- *social skills* (interpersonal intelligence) involved in working with and communicating to each other
- *cognitive skills* through having to explain, negotiate meanings and solve problems with each other
- *emotional support* through being motivated by the enthusiasm of the group or its leading members.

But these benefits do not arise simply by sitting children together. Research studies in British classrooms show that where children were seated in groups, most of their time was spent on individual tasks.[7] Typically children work in groups, but not *as* groups. Often sitting in groups positively distracts children from their work. Task-related talk is not always task enhancing. Typical exchanges included: 'Where are you up to? I'm on . . .', 'Can I borrow your rubber?', 'Do you have to underline?' Nor do children in groups necessarily get much teacher attention related to their learning. Much teacher time can be taken up in managing the group and organising resources. Children may also be left unsure about how much co-operation is allowed. When the teacher is present, group activity is high, but drops to around 50 per cent when the teacher is not actively engaged with the group. So what should be done?

One implication of these findings is that teachers should think carefully about the purpose of grouping children. Often there are no good grounds for sitting children in groups – they would work better on individual or paired tasks, sitting individually or in pairs. It may be relevant to have different groupings for different tasks. Children will need to sit in groups for genuinely co-operative group work. But what is genuinely co-operative group work, and how is it achieved?

Grouping children together is only justified if it helps to promote more effective learning, and results in co-operative activity that extends what the individual could do alone.

Ways of learning in groups

For co-operative groups to be successful, they have to be planned, supported and monitored. The children need to recognise the importance of working together, know the rules and sharing roles, have a clearly defined task, with agreed timescale, and criteria for success.

Ways of working in groups include:
- children working together on individual tasks, sitting in groups
- children working in a group on a shared task with a joint outcome, such as a problem-solving or construction task, or mapping their learning (see Chapter 5)
- children working together on different activities which contribute to a joint outcome, for example chapters of a story or a research task
- children working in a group with an adult who, for example, guides the learning of a small group through a planned series of tasks, or a larger group in a community of enquiry (see page 54).

The composition of groups

How should groups be composed? Do children learn better in groups of similar ability, or mixed ability? Research by Bennett and others indicates that groups of high ability children working together usually produced the most understanding and performance in group work.[8] Next in level of performance came mixed ability and average ability groups, with low ability groups working least well. High ability children tend to work well in whatever ability group they are put in. They work well together, and in mixed or low ability groups they often take the lead in explaining the task and organising the thinking of the group. The fear that high ability children miss out in mixed ability groups seems largely to be unfounded, if they are also given opportunities to work at optimal level with similar high ability children. They can gain by taking the 'teacher's role' in helping the group.

Tasks for group work

The important fact about group work is that it is not just a social experience, but should impose cognitive demands on the children involved. So what kinds of task are best suited for co-operative group work?

Activities suited to group working include:

- *Interpretative discussion* where groups investigate and discuss a given focus such as picture, poem or artefact – pooling ideas, sharing experiences or eliciting opinions, to interpret or describe what they have been given. Examples include: group reading, putting things in sequence (for example, cut-up lines of a poem), putting things in order of preference (such as pictures), putting things into sets (what will float /sink?).
- *Problem-solving tasks* where groups discuss an open-ended problem or situation, and decide between possible courses of action. Examples include: organising a fundraising event, solving an environmental or social problem, tackling a computer task, or preparing a group presentation.
- *Production tasks* where groups work in teams to produce a material outcome either by creating different prototypes and agreeing the best (as in designing a paper plane), or contributing different elements to a joint product (as in creating a newspaper or making a wall display to assist the class to research, for example Roman homes), or working on one large product (as in making a paper tower).

TASK 32

Group activities

Choose a topic or planned course of work in a curriculum area. Design one or more co-operative group activities for groups of your children that relates to the chosen topic or subject.

Try to create group activities for each of the following headings:

- interpretative discussion
- problem-solving
- production for display.

A useful distinction can be made between the two aspects of thinking that can contribute to a process of discussion – reflective thinking and active thinking (see Figure 7.3). These two aspects of thinking relate also to two aspects of group work, getting group members to reflect on how the group functioned as well as on the active outcome of the group effort. Questions to ask them to discuss include:

- How well did we work as a group?
- How successful was the outcome?

Planning for group work

Successful group work depends on good planning. Good advice is to start small, start simple and start structured. One way is to give pairs of children a simple task, like predicting the end of a story. Then put two pairs together to share ideas. This is useful for each pair has a contribution to make to the discussion. The group can then share with a larger group, such as a class. This strategy can be summed up as
Think–Pair–Group–Share

Key elements in planning for group work include:

- *Group size* – which size groups work best?
- *Group composition* – free choice, friendship, mixed or ability groups?
- *Group management* – what skills and strategies make for success?

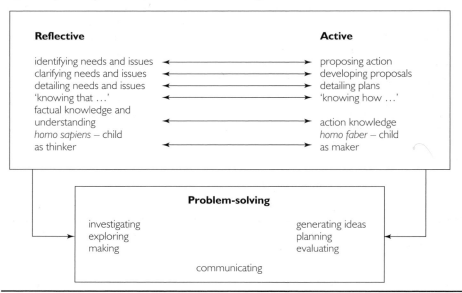

Reflective　　　　　　　　　　　　　　　**Active**

identifying needs and issues　⟵⟶　proposing action
clarifying needs and issues　⟵⟶　developing proposals
detailing needs and issues　⟵⟶　detailing plans
'knowing that …'　⟵⟶　'knowing how …'
factual knowledge and
understanding　⟵⟶　action knowledge
homo sapiens – child　　　*homo faber* – child
as thinker　⟵⟶　as maker

Problem-solving

investigating　　　　　　　generating ideas
exploring　　　　　　　　planning
making　　　　　　　　　evaluating

communicating

Figure 7.3 *Reflective and active thinking*[9]

Group size

The National Curriculum asks teachers to set up different groups for different tasks and purposes. Which is the best size for group work? Research suggests two answers to this:

- *no fixed rules*, with groups of three, four or five used for different tasks and purposes;
- *the rule of four*, which argues that groups of four allow for maximum communication between individuals, and that in groups of three or larger than four there are often outsiders.

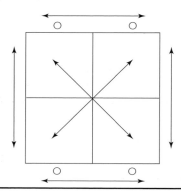

Figure 7.4 *The rule of four*[10]

Group composition

Two elements necessary for successful group work are security and challenge. Friendship groups offer students the greatest security, but not always the challenge needed to extend their thinking. Friendship groups also do not extend the social skills involved in relating to children they do not know or do not like. Success in life involves working at times with all sorts of people, and children should sometimes be persuaded to work in groups despite personal likes and dislikes. Mixed ability groups are likely to benefit the widest range of pupils, though opportunities should be given for those of similar ability, especially high attainers to work together.

Do children work better in gender or mixed-gender groups? Research findings provide no clear conclusions. Key factors seem to be the personalities of individual children, and the balance of skills in the group. Research shows that groups work best, irrespective of gender make-up, if they make good teams and have a blend of co-operative skills.[11]

Group work skills – team-building

Children need to be taught how to work in co-operative groups and to be made aware of the kinds of skills and behaviour that make learning in groups effective. Team building is necessary to help overcome the various problems associated with working together. Skills needed include the ability to:

- understand the needs of others and to take turns
- articulate a point of view
- listen to the viewpoint of others
- respond, question, discuss, argue and reason.

These skills are not in themselves innate. They have to be learnt. They can be divided into two kinds – the cognitive skills involved in processing information, and the social skills of working as a good team member.

Various barriers may need to be overcome. Barrier behaviours include being opinionated, aggressive, over-dominating, competitive, attention seeking, messing around, rejection of others and withdrawal. Groups will sometimes allow their 'stars' to do the work and make the decisions, and allow 'free riders' to opt out of all contributions. 'Stars', 'free riders' and other stereotypes can be identified in any group situation, staffroom or club.

The following activities help develop group work skills.

Who works or plays in group teams?
Children brainstorm different kinds of groups or teams, such as sports teams, factory teams, hospital teams, school teams, etc. List and share these. Choose one, for example a sports team. Discuss: What makes for good teamwork in this team?

Why work in a group?
Brainstorm with the students the reasons for working in a group.

For example, when a teacher of 6 year olds did this last task, the responses included:

- to practise getting on with one another
- to learn things other people know

- to get help with spellings
- to co-operate and help
- to listen to one another
- to think
- to solve problems
- to sort out what you will do.

What rules should there be?

Ask the children in groups to think of about six to 10 rules for working together. When these have been agreed children can make a group poster to show and share with others.

For example, these are the rules for discussion agreed by a group of 10 year olds:

1 Give everyone a turn at speaking.
2 Don't interrupt when someone else is talking.
3 Give support and help them add things.
4 Don't say anything stupid, mean or unpleasant.
5 If people don't want to say anything, they don't have to.
6 Don't laugh unkindly at something someone has said.
7 Think before you ask a question.

Can you make a group display?

Ask students to plan a display of work to which everyone in the group contributes, for example an art mural (try giving each member one element of the final design, such as one colour or one shape), a writing or research project, a music or movement presentation, a design or construction, or a puppet play.

Could you survive as a group on a desert island?

Groups imagine they have been shipwrecked on a desert island. What would they need to survive? What could each member of the group offer to do to help the others survive? What tasks would need doing? How would they share these tasks?

If they found a box washed ashore, what items would they most like to find in it to help them survive? (Agree on ten items, and try to list them in order of importance.) Compare lists.

Can your group give advice to help solve a problem?

Groups consider a problem that has been presented to them. They must discuss and try to agree a joint response to the problem. Examples of problems include common moral dilemmas such as: 'Two students find a £5 note in the street. What should they do with it?' or problems contributed (anonymously) by pupils themselves.

Can you read in a group?

Groups share reading aloud of a story or book, and discuss what they have read. Most students will need some guidance when asked to discuss a story, and it may be helpful to brainstorm a list of questions to help the group focus on the story, the illustrations and the way the story has been written.

TASK 33

Creating group rules

1 Ask groups of children to discuss, agree and write down all the rules they think will help the group to work well together.
2 Which rules do they think most important? Ask them to put the rules in order of priority.
3 Display and discuss the rules created by different groups.
4 Before a group task, check children know the rules by asking the groups: 'How will you know if you have worked well together?'
5 After a group task ask children to evaluate the quality of their collaboration against the rules. Should they change or modify the rules?

In 1811 Isaac Watts wrote:

> *If three or four persons agree to read the same book, and each brings his own remarks upon it, at some set hour appointed for the conversation, and they communicate mutually their sentiments on the subject, and debate about it in a friendly manner, this practice will render the reading of any author more abundantly beneficial to every one of them.*

As anyone who has had experience of organising group work will know, problems are almost bound to occur. Humans are social but not necessarily sociable animals. Some students may be 'group refusers'. Strategies to deal with these include:

- starting in pairs
- work for short periods of time
- reward good participation
- vary the groups
- allow the child to observe a group in action;
- try firm persuasion ('forcing the child' in Rousseau's phrase, 'to be free').

Over-quiet and over-dominating children may pose problems. Sometimes it helps to put the retiring child in a quiet group, and a 'dominant' child with an extrovert group. Success in group work means matching children to each other and the task to the group.

It can be helpful to assign different roles for members of a group, for example:

- *leader/chair* – organises the group, encourages participants and chairs the discussion
- *scribe* – notes main discussion points and any checks accuracy of notes with group
- *reporter* – presents a report summing up main points of discussion
- *mentor* – helps group members stay on task and keep to the agreed rules
- *observer* – notes how the group works, who contributed well, and reports back.

Another possible problem is that group members may demand individual attention from the teacher. One way to avoid excessive demands is to have the rule: *team questions only*. If the child has a question, she or he must first ask a member of the team. Only the spokesperson for the team may consult with another team. If, after trying, the team cannot find an answer, they may then ask the teacher the team question. The aim is to move the team from teacher-dependency to group independence or interdependence. As one teacher put it, 'I'll only help them if at first they've tried to help themselves.'

Remember the old advice: 'Keep 'em busy'. Give the group a specific task to undertake, in either verbal or written form. If you have set them an open task, have an alternative or extension activity ready, such as a checklist of things to discuss or a sequencing activity. If members of the group are going to have different roles such as chairperson, scribe, reporter, expert, sort this out beforehand. Make clear to them your own role in supporting, evaluating and rewarding their group effort. The aim is of course for the group to feel, 'We did it ourselves!'

Evaluating group work

Evaluating the process and outcomes of group work is important for students to monitor their co-operative behaviour and identify what they have learnt, and for teachers or others to assess what happened during the group work task and the outcomes of it.

The following questions can help children focus on different aspects of group work, and help promote the skills of self-evaluation:

- What do you think this work was about?
- What do you feel about what happened in your group today?
- What was good about your group work?
- What could have made it better?
- What do you think you have learnt?

The focus should be on what actually happened and on lessons learnt from the experience. For the teacher, the best ways of monitoring participation and progress is by a combination of:

- direct observation and note-taking (or listening to a tape-recording of group talk)
- discussion with individuals, with the group or with the class
- response from group members writing or drawing about the group task.

Assessment of group activity is made difficult by the complex interweaving of the social and cognitive aspects of learning. One child, asked to assess what he had learned from his group activity, replied, 'I haven't learnt much about building bridges but I now know how to stop Jason putting his hand up my bottom!' Many teachers are never without a notepad to record observations of students at work. It is advisable to focus on one group, or on the work of three or four children a week, trying to record key experiences and looking for the 'aha!' moments of learning breakthrough. Figure 7.5 is an example of an observation record sheet.

Learning in large groups

There are many benefits to be gained from learning in large groups – the traditional approach of organising and teaching children in classes. A large group or class is a community, and should provide the benefits of community support, resources and extended opportunities for learning. Research shows a link between successful learning in schools and high levels of effective whole-class teaching. What are the factors that make for success with children learning in large groups? Two aspects of the benefits of learning in a large group relate to the social/cultural context and the cognitive/intellectually challenging context.

Group work: observation record

Name: _____   Curriculum area: _____

Date: _____   Context for learning: _____

Observations:

_____

_____

Figure 7.5 Observation record

The social/cultural context

The ethos of standards and expectations created and maintained by the community, school or class can become reflected to a greater or lesser extent in the individual learner. A community or a school can create a powerful learning environment (see page 136), which will exert a strong influence on the learner. A large group context should provide the essential structure, purpose and control needed for learning to flourish.

The cognitive/intellectually challenging context

The intellectual stimulus to challenge and extend the child involves the use of 'higher order questioning, explanations and statements, and these in turn correlate with higher levels of pupil performance' particularly in the basic subjects. Such teaching should aim to involve *all* the pupils in active thinking and responding.[12]

Not that active thinking is always seen as a good thing. As one child recently said after his class had been brainstorming for some time, 'Can't I get on by myself, all this thinking makes my brain hurt!' But another child's response was, 'I like this thinking together, 'cos it helps you think more.'

Summary

Each child is an individual and has individual learning needs. However, most human learning is a social process, with others involved in co-operative activity with the learner. Successful learning in groups requires a communicative framework. This can be achieved through co-operative work in pairs, for example in reading or writing activities. Co-operative learning can be undertaken through discussion, problem-solving or production tasks. Important considerations for effective group work include not only the activities to be undertaken, but also the composition of groups and the development of group working skills. Children also benefit from learning in large groups. Research into co-operative learning supports the view that effective group work develops both the social and cognitive aspects of learning.

8 Coaching learning

How cognitive coaching can support learning

*In his teaching the wise man guides his students but does not pull them along; he urges them to
go forward and does not suppress them; he opens the way but does not take them to the place …
if his students are encouraged to think for themselves we may call the man a good teacher.*

Confucius (*c.* fifth century BC)

*The best sort of teacher is one who helps you do what you couldn't do by yourself, but doesn't do
it for you.*

Ravi, aged 8

Ask a group of people where they study best and you usually get a variety of responses
– at a desk, lying on the floor, by oneself, with others, in silence, talking with others,
in short bursts, for a length of time, and so on. Thinking and learning is an idiosyn-
cratic process. We all have our own unique learning style, and what works for us in one
situation may not suit us in another. As the philosopher Whitehead reminds us: 'Each
human being is a more complex structure than any social system to which he belongs'.[1]
It is this complexity, this many-layered functioning, this variability of response that
makes the task of teaching and of matching levels of support to the needs of individual
students so challenging. All children need support as learners, but they don't always
know what support they need or where to get it. This chapter looks at some general
principles of cognitive coaching, and at teaching strategies that can help children learn
in a wide range of contexts.

There are occasions when students learn well in large groups and in small groups. But at
some time all benefit from being taught in a one-to-one situation where the teacher:

- gives individual help in learning
- shows students how to take responsibility for their own learning.

All learners need some individual interaction with a teacher, some short period of time
set aside when the teacher's attention is focused specifically on the needs of that individual. Research shows that this is a rare occurrence in busy classrooms, and some
children – often the quiet ones who get on with their work – get by with very little
individual attention. They are the 'invisible children' that exist in almost every class. If
you know of a class of children, can you think who the 'invisible children' might be?

Individual children will need different kinds of help, for example being shown a technique, given a word of advice or encouragement, or told information that will help
them in their work. Cognitive coaching is giving learners a special kind of help. It is
help that is generative, aimed at giving them more than knowledge in a routine fact-
giving sense, but to develop those open capacities that help them transfer their
learning to other situations. Cognitive coaching can be summed up as teaching for
transfer, seeking to teach the individual student transferable skills of learning.[2]

Cognitive apprenticeship

It was only during the nineteenth century that the idea arose that it might be approp-riate to send all children to school, for a period of time. Not until the twentieth century did we come to believe that all children should stay in school through adolescence and that school came to have the prime role of preparing children for life. In previous gen-erations, children were largely taught in family settings and in apprenticeships. Despite limitations, the apprenticeship system had some important advantages over school. It taught skills in the context of actual work. Skills did not remain abstract abil-ities, but were applied as knowledge in use.

One of the problems with school-learning is that it teaches skills that do not seem directly related to everyday life or the student's needs. A learner needs not only declarative knowledge (knowing the facts of the matter) and procedural knowledge (skills and know-how), but also *applied knowledge*, about where, when and how to apply particular skills and procedures. Applied knowledge is the kind embedded in a human context, and in the particularity of human life. For example, many studies have shown that although the 'four rules' of mathematics (addition, subtraction, multiplication and division) are known, many students cannot see how to use them in solving simple everyday problems.

Evidence suggests that there are students leaving school in a state of conceptual con-fusion about some of the basic concepts of maths, science, history and other key areas of learning, for they have not learnt how to apply their knowledge. It is not surprising that schools, when burdened by the demands of a heavy and abstract curriculum, become disappointing environments for learning.

The following extract from a conversation with a young child reveals the roots of a lack of cognitive understanding about mathematics:

RF: Why are you working with numbers?
Child: [*working on a mathematics workbook*] To colour them in.
RF: But why are you adding those numbers up?
Child: Because we have to do them.
RF: Is it a good thing to learn how to add up?
Child: Yes
RF: Why?
Child: Because the teacher tells you to.
RF: Who else uses numbers?
Child: I don't know.
RF: Have you seen anyone else using numbers?
Child: Mary.
RF: What does Mary do with numbers?
Child: [*Pointing to a child on another table*] She colours them in.

The cognitive apprenticeship approach means placing a much greater value on intellec-tual processes than the sort of production line 'busy work', such as filling in worksheets, that is a characteristic of some classes. It introduces into school many of the features that made traditional apprenticeships effective, by encouraging students to be engaged in dis-ciplined and productive mental work such as in the past were applied to craft activities. Three key elements in the effective teaching of apprenticeship are challenge, context and coaching. Cognitive apprenticeship works best when students are engaged on:

- *challenging tasks* which require mental effort, such as reading a text that takes some effort to understand, writing to persuade an audience, or investigating a mathematical or scientific problem which encourages students to think for themselves
- *contextualised tasks* which have a purpose, such as writing for an interested audience, reading for information, or applying mathematical or scientific knowledge to real-world problems
- *coached tasks* which aim to assist learning, such as observing others do what they will be expected to learn, seeing models of effective performance, and being shown standards by which to judge their own performance.

Cognitive coaching need not be time-consuming. Work with one child might take 2 or 3 minutes, but if it is based on the principles of cognitive coaching, it will have contributed to learning and to the child's ability to learn. The ideal is to make cognitive coaching a flexible part of the daily routine. A concern for all teachers is 'How can I find time to work with one child in a room with more than 20 children needing my attention?' One answer is that cognitive coaching need not be a separate activity but part of the regular teaching pattern of the day. Another approach is to set aside a planned time of coaching for every individual child over a period of time, for example once a week or fortnight. As one teacher put it, 'It means turning some of my routine teaching into "quality-time" teaching.'

Some of the models for cognitive coaching have been inspired by the ideas of Vygotsky, who argued that children develop particular cognitive capacities through collaboration with expert practitioners. At first, the child is a spectator of the activity of someone who is more expert (for example, a teacher, parent or older sibling). The child as novice takes over some of the work under the supervision of the expert, and is gradually given more responsibility in the activity until eventually the child takes full responsibility for performing the task, with the expert as a supportive audience. Using this approach children learn about the task at an assisted pace, joining in when they can. The gap between which the child can manage independently and the level which the child can reach with expert help Vygotsky called the *zone of proximal (or potential) development*. Vygotsky claimed that 'what children can do with the assistance of others might be in some sense even more indicative of their mental development than what they can do alone'.[3]

Research into the differences between good and poor learners shows that good learners tend to:

- focus and concentrate on tasks in hand
- generate questions about their learning
- monitor and resolve problems as they occur
- translate what they are learning into verbal and visual images
- persevere when they fail at part of a task.

While poor learners tend to:

- lack the ability to focus on the task in hand
- lack a clear idea of the purpose of learning
- lack awareness of the skills needed to be successful at learning
- view learning as a passive activity which you either can or cannot do
- give up easily on learning tasks.

The aim for teachers is to devise ways in which poor learners can practise the strategies of good learners. One way is to ask children to think about what they do when engaged on a learning activity, such as reading. For example, they might reply, 'I miss out a word I don't know', 'I get a picture in my mind' or 'If I don't understand it I read it again more slowly'. The teacher could then display these strategies in the classroom, so that poorer readers/learners can be made aware of the strategies used by better readers. 'Simplify . . . simplify', advised Thoreau, and it is by concentrating and making children aware of simple strategies that we can avoid complications and cognitive confusion.

TASK 34

Reflecting on thinking and learning

Do your children think they are good thinkers and learners? What do they think makes good thinkers and learners? One way to find out what they think is to ask them questions such as:

1 Can you draw (or give examples of) someone who is a good thinker/learner? Can you draw (or give examples of) someone who is not a good thinker/learner
2 Do you think you are a good thinker/learner? Why do you think so?
3 What can help people to be good thinkers/learners? What stops some people being good thinkers/learners?

Strategies for cognitive coaching

There has been much research into effective ways of cognitive coaching,[4] and into the problems of poor learners. The following seven strategies have been found to be effective in coaching for thinking and learning:

- focusing
- explaining
- scaffolding
- modelling
- follow-throughs: questions and repeats
- reciprocal teaching
- summarising
- positive feedback.

Focusing

One of the recurrent complaints of teachers is, 'Why don't they concentrate?' The complaints of confused learners include, 'Where do you begin?' and 'What do I do now?' Strategies of coaching that aim to address these problems include focusing and 'follow-throughs'. In focusing, we try to direct the student's attention to the important features of the problem or learning situation. We are not simply telling them what to look at or think about, but require them to tell us what the central focus of attention should be. Focusing and follow-throughs aim to help children to take more time, to attend more closely and to hold the focus of attention sufficiently long enough to allow thinking processes to work. They are scaffolding questions in which the hidden (or spoken) message is to 'Look at it again' and 'Think about it more'.

Focusing is part of cognitive coaching when it makes a cognitive demand on the child. It makes a positive cognitive intervention by creating a double focus:

- a perceptual focus on what the situation is about
- a conceptual demand for the child to say what they think it means.

Focusing, which encourages the selective attention of the child, needs to be followed-up by challenges that will sustain attention. With young children and poor learners, attention tends to be erratic and is easily diverted from the task in hand. The aim is to sustain attention by making appropriate cognitive demands on the child. There are a number of ways to help children practise focusing and sustaining their attention. Meditation has long been recognised as a valuable tool for developing powers of concentration, calming of the mind and in creating a receptive state.[5] Begin by asking children to listen, in absolute silence, to distant sounds. Sustain this at first for half a minute, then up to a minute or more with practice. My research into the uses of meditation with children shows that it can have long-term effects. When I met an ex-pupil many years after I had taught him in school, I asked what he remembered from his days, 20 years before, in my class. He replied (after a rather long pause), 'I remember when we sat there – and did nothing!' He remembered the meditation I had taught them and said he still practised it when he needed to still his mind.

Other ways to focus attention include the use of music, aerobic activity (for example Brain Gym) or quick mental quizzes. Any activity that requires intense focus helps prepare the mind for learning by overriding all the busy thoughts and concerns that may be preoccupying the mind and diverting attention. The optimum mental state for learning is one of relaxed attention. The following are some focus exercises to try:

- *Circle pats* – children circle their stomach with the right hand and with the left hand pat their heads, then they change hands and reverse the circling.
- *Long limb stretches* – stretch slowly and rotate arms, shoulders and legs in turn.
- *Making faces* – yawn, grimace, make silly faces, silent chuckles and big smiles.

Explaining

Every day millions of people coach others through explanation. Effective explanation has certain characteristics in common, whether it is a policeman giving directions to a tourist, a garage mechanic explaining what is wrong with a car engine or a mother warning her children about strangers. Some people get it right by getting to the heart of the matter, using the right words, giving appropriate examples at just the right level of understanding. Other explanations only serve to confuse, and offer no structure that we can comprehend.

Children recognise and value clear explanations. We have all experienced the benefits of having things clearly explained and also of explanations that simply add to our confusion and puzzlement. What are the characteristics of effective explanation? The following are some of the features of good explanations identified in research.[6]

Clear structure

In every situation, there are certain key elements or central ideas. It is often best to give the key idea first. Be clear about the distinct nature of the key concepts (make sure you have a good grasp of the main ideas). Aid clarity and comprehensibility of your explanation by:

- *remembering the 'rule of three'* – three linked ideas are a powerful combination: 'There are three things I want you to remember . . .'
- *repeating key ideas* – remember the old advice: 'Say what you are going to say, say it and say what you have said'
- *reviewing the links between the main ideas* – link a clear opening with a closing review (which can be a summary by teacher or pupil).

Simple language

The key to being understood is to keep it simple. Before giving an important speech, an invited speaker was passed a card by his wife. On it she had simply written 'KISS'. Afterwards he said to his wife how charmed he had been by her loving note. 'Loving nothing', she said. 'It stood for "Keep It Simple Stupid".' Keep the language simple, and learners are more likely to understand the message.

Varied presentation

Maintain interest by use of varied voice, gesture and focus of attention. Use voice and body to sustain interest. Avoid monotony or too much variety of approach. Illustrate your explanation with examples, particularly ones which relate to the learners' existing knowledge and interests. Try to cater for different learning styles – the audiles who like to listen to questions and to be given narrative examples (such as an illustrative anecdote); the visiles who like visual stimulus such as graphic examples and the kinaesthetic who like practical activities. Enliven explanation with analogy and humour. Amend explanation in light of feedback from learners.

Fluency

Clarity is maintained by simplicity, interest by variety and fluency by pace. Pacing is important. However what is really important in pace is not interactive pace (getting through a lot of stuff quickly) but cognitive pace (keeping up the momentum of challenge and interest). One way to keep the momentum going is to communicate enthusiasm and a genuine interest in the topic. Another is to break up long explanations with questions or activities that check the learners' understanding. As one child put it, 'I like my teacher she never stops . . . she only stops to make us think.'

These features can be summed up as *instructional clarity*. Teacher clarity is consistently associated with student achievement, and is one of the behaviours most often identified by students listing the characteristics of their most effective teachers, for example:

- 'She takes time to explain things, so you always understand what you have to do.'
- 'She always asks if there are any questions, and goes over things.'
- 'He puts it into words you can understand.'

According to George Washington, 'Actions, not words, are the true criterion.' Sometimes students find it hard to act on the most patient and careful of explanations; they come to understand better by being shown by someone more able than themselves than by being told. Actions sometimes speak louder and tell us more than words.

Scaffolding

Inexperienced learners learn from working with others who are more expert. With the help of others, we can do more than we can do on our own. When others help, but do not do it all themselves, they provide a 'scaffold' on which learners can build their own ideas and understanding. Gradually the learner is encouraged to take over more and more of the task until they can do it without assistance. They are then ready to take on more demanding challenges, again assisted by the scaffolding of an expert. Thus in learning we move from dependence to independence, increasing our expertise through assisted practice. This, according to Vygotsky, is how children learn 'naturally' within families and communities.

Scaffolding involves offering the learner support when they are faced with understanding ideas or learning new skills. This support may come through explanation or modelling (see next section), by providing frameworks (such as a rule or recipe) or giving prompts (clues which lead the way to success). Scaffolding is a form of guided practice. One teacher expressed it thus:

> To get to a new place we need a guide, to remember the way we need to practise, then we need to try it for ourselves. Each of these stages is equally important.

Recognising when to withdraw the scaffolding or guideline is important if children are not to become over-dependent on the help provided by others. The aim is independent learning. As someone once said, education is what you remember when you have forgotten what you have been taught. Teaching should be merely be the scaffolding needed for independent learning. We need to provide the verbal and visual supports, such as cue cards, summary charts or thinking frames. Growing independence in learning means the learner deciding what help is needed, and when (or if) to use it. 'What do you do when you are stuck?' is a key question for any learner. Asking children to reflect on the strategies they need to use is an essential part of helping them to scaffold their own learning. As Peter, aged eight, said when grappling with a problem, 'Don't tell me, let me try for myself, then if I'm wrong . . . give me a clue.'

Modelling

Teacher: Why do you think Robert Frost repeated the last line of this verse?
Student: [*No response*]
Teacher: [*After a long pause*] Well, what feelings did you have as you read the poem?
Student: Why don't you just tell us the answer?

Students often resist the invitation to think for themselves. It is easier for them to be told than to think. How do we convey that the goal of learning is think for oneself? A powerful strategy for assisting learning is being an example or model of the process you are teaching.

Imitation is probably the chief means of learning new behaviour. Indeed it is so strong that one of the problems of maturity is developing the ability to resist imitating others. Children are socialised largely through imitating the unconscious acts of others. Traditional cultures were largely handed down through demonstration and modelling rather than verbal explanation. In modern times, research into modelling shows that children acquire much of their behaviour, habits, values and many of their thinking frames, not from direct instruction but through imitating adult and peer models.[7] Modelling, to be effective, requires more than simple mimicry. Modelling needs to be structured for understanding so that it can be transformed into images and verbal guides to subsequent performance. No amount of looking at a chess master or great painter will necessarily help in your own performance of these tasks. However if we are able to actively code the components of behaviour through watching others then we can be helped to learn and retain complex skills.

Modelling involves performing an action or series of actions that can be processed in the learner's mind. It is an important means of assisting performance for it is often difficult in words to convey all the information that can be included in a visual or live demonstration. In particular, learners whose conceptual and verbal skills are underdeveloped often benefit more from physical demonstration than from verbal explanation as a means of showing learning in action.

Extended contact with a child gives a teacher opportunities to become a significant and influential model in that child's life. If emulation of others is a basic way of learning, then exhibiting desired kinds of behaviour can be a strong influence on students. This example can be shown in two aspects of modelling. The first is in the general 'teaching for thinking' behaviours that infuse all areas of the curriculum. For example:

- If listening to one another is valued, the teacher listens actively and with full attention to students.
- If taking time to think is valued, the teacher must take time to wait and think about problems or the answers of students.
- If allowing other points of view is important, the teacher must invite, consider and value different points of view.
- If 'thinking things through' is important, the teacher should model 'thinking aloud' when working on tasks or problems.
- If curiosity and questioning are of value, the teacher must share their enthusiasm for discovery and their wonder at the world.

Modelling has also been found to be effective in supporting specific areas of the curriculum. The teacher of reading who wishes to give value to the practice of reading will model the reading process, not only by sharing in the child's experience of books but also by showing that she or he reads books for enjoyment and information. Many teachers have a regular quiet reading time in class, sometimes called USSR (Uninterrupted Sustained Silent Reading) or ERIC (Everyone Reading in Class) in which the children and the teacher read books of their own choice. As one teacher says, 'If reading is important I want to show my children the pleasure and value I get out of it. We all become part of the same reading club.' Novice readers are encouraged to join in the process at a level they can manage, and which includes some experience of reading performance at a higher level. By behaving in many ways as if the desired levels of knowledge and skill were actual, novices are treated as if they are competent in the processes they engage in. In so doing they move towards full participation in the community of readers.

Whatever the subject-matter of teaching, whether maths, science, music, art or social studies, we can invite children into that particular club by showing how we, at an adult level, participate in those activities at our own level. Apprenticeship learning is made more powerful when we make explicit the rules of thought and relate them to the kinds of task we are engaged in. Having identified the thinking skill or process, we can teach it directly by:

- *introducing the skill* – for example, how to find something in an index
- *explaining the skill* – saying why the information is important
- *modelling the skill* – showing how you do it
- *reviewing what was done* – ask them to tell you what you did
- *reflecting on the use* – where else the skill can be applied.

Teachers of skills from physical education to art have long used demonstration as a primary mode of teaching. These demonstrations are given added value when linked to the thinking skills that make for successful performance and appraisal. The best sort of modelling is when teachers take on the role of intelligent novices. They model performance at a slightly higher, more coherent and informed level than is characteristic of their children. To do this, it is helpful to focus on a particular cognitive strategy and provide a model to assist the children in using that strategy. For example, a teacher wanting children to refer to evidence in an information book modelled the following 'think alouds' as she made a systematic search of the book:

I am trying to find out something about Henry VIII's wives. I am looking in the Contents page and seeing if I can see anything . . . I can't see a chapter on Henry VIII's wives . . . but I'm not going to give up. I'm going to look up the index . . . it's at the back. It's alphabetical so I look down the list until I get to Henry . . . doesn't seem to mention his wives . . . so I'm going to search through the pages (turns pages) . . . Ah, here's a picture of someone who may be his wife . . . let's look at the caption . . . Anne Boleyn . . . can we find that name on the page?

TASK 35
Modelling
Practise role modelling in a chosen subject area. Use the opportunity to share with children something you are currently learning from your own adult experience. Share any pleasures or problems that arise, expressing these at their level of understanding. This is one way of doing this task
1   Choose a book for information or pleasure that you enjoy reading.
2   Find time to read this during a time when your children are also reading their chosen books.
3   After the reading session, tell the children about your book, how you came to choose it and what you have learnt or enjoyed about it.
4   Invite questions about your book.
5   Ask the children to show and tell about their books.

When children live with criticism,
They learn to condemn.

When children live with hostility,
They learn to fight.

When children live with ridicule,
They learn to be shy.

When children live with shame,
They learn to feel guilty.

When children live with tolerance,
They learn to be patient.

When children live with encouragement,
They learn confidence.

When children live with security,
They learn to have faith.

When children live with fairness,
They learn justice.

When children live with praise,
They learn to appreciate.

When children live with approval,
They learn to like themselves.

When children live with acceptance and friendship,
They learn to find love in the world.

Figure 8.1 Children live by what they learn

Follow-throughs: questions and repeats

The skill in coaching is to match the cognitive demand to the ability of the child. Where there is no challenge, no mental effort, then no new learning will take place. It will simply be a rehearsal of what is known. An able child summed this up by saying about his teacher, 'She's boring. She doesn't do anything that you don't already know.' But if the challenge is too great, and beyond the child's repertoire of skills this will lead to frustration and disaffection. Challenge needs, therefore, to be structured and sequential, moving from the simple to the complex, from the concrete to the abstract, from lower to higher levels of thinking. The demands for initial focusing should be extended by follow-through questions which sustain attention, making progressively greater demands on the child within the limits of their competence.

The following illustrate some examples of questions that can be used to make increasing demands on levels of attention and thinking:

- *Labelling* – What is it? What is it called? What are you doing?
- *Application* (simple functions) – What do you do with it? What is it for?
- *Memory* – Have you said/done this before?
- *Description* – Tell me about it. What is happening? What does it look like?
- *Selective perception* – What else can you see? What is this part like? What is the problem?
- *Refocusing perception* – Find me the part . . . Where can you see? Show me where . . .
- *Reasoning about perception* – Why is it like that? Which is the most important part? What is missing?
- *Comparative analysis* – How are these parts similar? How are they different?
- *Cause and effect* – What has made this happen/caused this? What will happen/will be the effect?
- *Predicting/hypothesising* – What will happen next? What will happen if . . . ?
- *Means–end relationships* – What can you/I do to achieve the goal/solve the problem? What is needed? Why? How can it be done?
- *Informal reasoning* – How do you know? How can you be sure? What are your reasons?
- *Logical relationships* – If . . . then . . . ? What are the implications?
- *Assessing parts* – Which parts are good? Which part is best? What would you change?
- *Evaluating wholes* – What do you think of it (as a whole)? How would you compare it with others? What could make it better?[8]

Research into reading shows the value of helping children to refocus, and to follow-through or process information for understanding. A simple yet very important strategy is to reread a text to gain more information and understanding of it. Other simple strategies include retelling or summarising a story. Less able readers sometimes don't know that retelling is a matter of summing up rather than resaying every part, or that you can skim rather than reread every word to pick out the most important points. They are not aware that the first and last sentences of a paragraph are often particularly important in understanding what the passage is about. Other successful strategies of good readers include questioning and discussing to clarify the meanings in what they read. They also tend to predict what will come next in the text, and this adds pleasure and expectation to reading. Younger and less able children know less about themselves, the tasks they face and the strategies they employ. One approach that aims to teach these learning strategies is called reciprocal teaching.

Reciprocal teaching

Reciprocal teaching is the name given to an apprenticeship approach which is a kind of interactive game between the teacher and learner, with each taking it in turns to lead in teaching the other.[9] It follows the old principle that to teach is to learn twice, and the best way for children to learn a process is to get them to teach it. The process was initially designed to help children with reading and comprehension difficulties to practise the strategies used by successful learners. It consists of four activities:

- *summarising* – asking children to summarise the text or what they have learnt, encouraging them to focus on the main ideas of the passage or process, and to check their understanding of these
- *questioning* – getting children to ask questions about what they have read or learnt, encouraging attention to main ideas and to think about their own comprehension of these
- *clarifying* – asking children to clarify any problematic areas of text or understanding, requiring them to critically evaluate the current state of their understanding
- *predicting* – getting them to go beyond the text and present state of affairs to make inferences and to justify these from clues given in the content or structure of the text.

These activities have a dual role: a cognitive function in asking children to work on the comprehension of a given text or learning task, and a metacognitive function in challenging their ability to reflect on their own levels of comprehension. The procedure is to take turns in leading the discussion about a particular section of text or task. The teacher first models the process by summarising, asking a question, clarifying a point and predicting what will come next. Next time round the child takes on one or more of these activities, where posssible, and gradually expands this role. The aim is to gradually remove assistance to the learner, encouraging the learner to take more responsibility in the learning situation. Children with learning difficulties find it hard to take responsibility for learning and to adopt the role of teacher, but with experience of modelling and help in verbalising they can undertake and practise some of the comprehension and monitoring activities of more able learners.

With struggling learners, it is useful to break the task down into small steps, for example by breaking up the text to be read into paragraphs. It is a good idea to make the process explicit, saying what you are doing and why, and rehearsing the process. Reciprocal teaching is useful for small group activity because the children can model for each other the processes involved. Introduce students to the 'language' and process of reciprocal teaching by describing and practising each strategy. When asked how someone becomes good at reading, a child responded, 'I don't know, you either can do it or you can't.' The goal of using strategies like scaffolding, modelling and follow-through questions and repeats is to demystify the learning process, so that children are given greater control rather than being baffled by classroom experiences.

Summarising

Summarising is one of the strategies of reciprocal teaching and it is a useful coaching strategy in a wide variety of contexts. It is what we ask children to do whenever we ask questions such as 'What did you do in school today?', 'What did we do in the last lesson?', 'How are you going to plan your project?' Summarising is important in specific teaching contexts, such as reading. A useful rule of thumb in assessing reading is that if a reader cannot summarise a text, it is too hard or it needs to be reread. Woody Allen tells the story of when he took a speed-reading course, and read Tolstoy's *War and Peace*. When asked what it was about, he replied, 'It's about Russia.'

Summarising is an excellent means of synthesising the meaning of a complex message. It is useful as a process of review and as a prelude to evaluation. The ability to provide a good summary is an advanced, higher order skill. It involves a number of important cognitive processes[10] including:

- judging which ideas are important
- applying rules for condensing information
- practising in the communication of key ideas.

Summarising can be done as spoken or written summary, and older children should gain experience of both. The practice of taking notes and concept mapping can help in this process. As these are advanced skills, plenty of guided practice is needed. Students will need to be shown what to do and told the strategies that will help them, such as:

- deleting unnecessary material
- grouping parts into larger concepts
- picking out key terms, phrases or sentences
- creating new sentences which summarise the important points.

Children should be encouraged to 'look for the big ideas' in all that they learn. A good way to begin is for the teacher to model the process, and for the teacher to think aloud while searching for the main ideas. The following are some activities to help in develop the skills of summarising.

TASK 36

Summarising

These activities are for the teacher to model, and then for students to try.

1 Read a passage from a chosen book and summarise its main idea.
2 Retell a chosen story (such as a popular fairy tale) in the shortest number of words.
3 Write a chosen story as a short newspaper report. Try editing it down to 40 words, then down to 20 words.

The teacher or coach has structures of understanding that are not available to the pupil. Cognitive structures are the thinking frames through which we regulate our lives and the lives of others. One of the problems children face when entering school is to get into the thinking frames of school life. Every task that children face has its own set of thinking frames. Often these frames are implicit, like the rules of a game. For example, for cooking the thinking frames might include knowledge of foodstuffs, use of cooking utensils, rules of safety and procedures appropriate for particular recipes. As one child said during a cookery session, trying to remember all the rules, 'What I'm learning in cooking is how to boil my brains!' For novices it takes mental effort to bring thinking frames to mind, to form them into the right sets and patterns and to apply them appropriately. Without cognitive structures, the child's response to the world becomes random and haphazard.

Some cognitive structures are universal, such as the constants of time and space. Some structures are general, in that they apply to a wide range of experiences. Proverbs function as one way in which social experience is generalised. Some structures function as specific instructions, such as the cognitive structure for writing – full stop, then capital letter. These structures help children to organise their ideas, and apply them as rules in like instances. They begin as rules or recipes and gradually become internalised as automatic procedures. Other kinds of thinking frame help to structure cognitive activity, they are not so much instructions or explanations as calls to action, such as, 'In every story try to find the main idea'.

Most researchers make a distinction between these two types of cognitive structure:

- *structures of explanation*, for example 'every story has a main idea'
- *structures for cognitive activity*, for example 'always try to find the main idea'.

Both kinds of structure are important. Coaching that relies only on one type of structure, for example content instruction or process activity may be missing an important element of learning. Theory and practice, explanation and activity, structure and process are united in the informed action that is the hallmark of effective learning. This book has discussed various general strategies of cognitive activity that promote learning. These are structures that promote cognitive activity. Equally important are the structures of explanation. Good teaching can be seen as a combination or blending of effective explanation linked to cognitive activity. What is effective explanation?

Positive feedback – during performance

I like what you are doing. Do you know why?
    Teacher to child

We all welcome praise when we feel it is honestly given and is deserved. Research studies have shown that teachers tend to blame more than they praise, and notice faults more readily than they do virtues. Effort thrives on praise. Children need feedback on their past efforts and feedforward to help them identify what will make for future success and further praise.

Feeding back during performance is a powerful means of assisting learning. (For more on assessment after learning, see Chapter 9.) Thanks to research we are now in a good position to identify the features that make for effective feedback. Feedback can take many forms, such as teacher response, test data, self-assessment, and so on, but to be effective it must be guided by criteria of judgement, consistency of application and proximity of response to performance. The problem with feedback in the classroom is that it can often be inconsistent or too remote to be useful. Feedback is a term derived from cybernetics, the study of information systems. It does not refer to random information travelling along unconnected lines. For information to be feedback, it implies the existence of a closed loop that includes criteria by which performance can be judged against standards. It is important therefore to be explicit about the criteria being used and the standards that are being aimed for. How are these standards to be set?

One way of providing standards is to offer models. For example, the teacher can offer a model of good performance, or students can see and study good models achieved by other students. One teacher, for example, will often show her children as a prelude to their activity an example of a child's work – without saying whether it is a good or bad example. The work may be a piece of writing in a writing lesson, artwork in an art lesson or way of tackling a problem in a maths lesson. She will then ask children to judge (provide feedback) on the work, for example by saying 'Can you find two good things about this . . . (piece of work)?' and 'Can you say one way in which it can be improved?'

The important aspects of feedback are that:

- children should not feel that success is too easy, or too difficult, to achieve
- they should know what standards to aim for, and the criteria by which to judge their own work and the work of others
- praise of children's work should be specific and relate to both process and performance, for example 'I like the way you tried different methods to find the answer, and well done for getting the right answer.'

When Confucius was told that Chi Wen Tzu used to think thrice before acting, he replied: 'Twice is enough.' To optimise challenge and avoid frustration, there must be feedback and review of performance. Feedback during performance allows the chance to correct errors, and also to motivate students by giving them a sense of success, and reasssuring them that they are building on competent work. Forms of feedback include verbal praise, awards and rewards. The best forms of motivation are intrinsic, and stem from children's own belief in what they do. The most potent forms of feedback give learners a justified belief in themselves, in their capacity to learn and to review their own progress.

The good coach is like the wise ruler described in the ancient Chinese text *Tao teh Ching*:

The wisest rulers the people do not notice,
the next best they cherish and praise,
the next best they fear,
and the next best they revile.
For if trust is found lacking,
trust is not given.
The wise ruler treasures his words,
and when the work is done
the people say: 'We did it ourselves!'

Summary

Coaching refers to a range of strategies used to assist learning and to counter the conceptual confusions of learners. Coaching aims to create the conditions of cognitive apprenticeship, which include providing optimal challenge, purposeful contexts and assistance in performance of learning tasks. Ways of assisting performance include focus and follow-through questions, reciprocal teaching, summarising, explaining, modelling and positive feedback. Success in coaching does not depend on any one method, but a range of approaches that unite curriculum and cognitive aims, and meet the different needs and learning styles of students. The ultimate aim of the coach is to create independent learners who have the capacity to coach themselves and others.

9 Reviewing and assessing learning

Reviewing and assessing progress can support self-esteem and learning.

A person who doubts himself is like a man who would enlist in the ranks of his enemies and bears arms against himself. He makes his failure certain by himself being the first person to be convinced of it.

   Alexandre Dumas (*The Three Musketeers*, 1844)

If I think I can do something, I can usually do it. When I don't think I can do it, I usually fail.

   Elyn, aged 12

One day an English class was asked to do something surprising. They had been given a number of co-operative tasks to undertake in small groups. These included: listing as many things present in the room as they could in 1 minute, and identifying in their list what they thought would not appear on any other list; noting the possible uses of a paper clip; discussing famous people they would like to meet and ranking the top five; and sorting strip cartoon pictures into the right order. The lesson ended with a task that was in many ways the most challenging. The students were asked to write down what they thought they had learned from the lesson. Some of these reviews began as follows:

- From this lesson, I've learnt that you have to work in a group to achieve certain things . . .
- I think this lesson was quite good. It made us think of things quickly . . .
- I think this lesson was well worth having, because of the pleasure it brought me . . .[1]

What was new to the students was that they were not being treated simply as passive recipients of teaching, but were being regarded as active reviewers of their own learning. This process of review can help build self-esteem, self-awareness and provides a useful focus for thinking about learning.

Self-esteem

One factor in the possible success or failure of any human endeavour is that precious source of energy known as *self-esteem*. This is true of learning as in other areas of life. If children develop a sense of inadequacy in themselves as learners they will live self-fulfilling prophecies like 'I cannot learn . . .', 'I am not capable . . .', 'I am no good at anything'. They will not develop a positive sense of self-worth and self-competence, but rather what has been called 'learned helplessness'.[2]

Children who do not have a positive view of themselves as active learners will look elsewhere for sources of self-respect. Studies have shown that self-esteem is not related to family, education, wealth, geographical location, social class, father's occupation or having a mother at home. It comes from relationships with those who play a significant role in the child's life. It is formed by the person's assessment of the 'self pictures' that are daily reflected back from others.

Self-esteem is the quiet inner knowing that we are all right, that our worth is recognised by others as well as by ourselves. It is a sense of self-respect, a feeling of self-worth, a knowledge of who we are and what we can do. The main sources of this feeling come from:

- affirmation of positive qualities from parents, teachers and other significant carers
- recognition from peers, siblings and other children
- self-belief based on their own experiences of competence and success.

Children value themselves as learners to the degree that they have been valued. To focus on achievement in learning without also focusing on building self-esteem is only to half educate a child. Research has consistently shown a correlation between self-esteem and achievement in reading, writing, maths and other subjects.[3] It is an area no teacher or parent can afford to neglect. It is often a necessary, though not sufficient, condition for success. Self-esteem by itself is not enough for it can encourage an uncritical self-satisfaction. What is needed is to link self-esteem to self-awareness and to create in children what has been called *mastery orientation*.

Mastery orientation

Mastery orientation refers to a sense of self-competence or self-efficacy that children develop from an early age and that moulds their approach to learning. It is the 'can do' attitude of 'I am good at tasks and know how to do them'. Children who are mastery oriented are curious, they want to learn, and in particular they have developed the resilience to cope with failure and frustration. Mastery orientation makes for success in learning, in particular the ability to respond to challenges, the urge to succeed in handling problems and learning tasks. Mastery orientation often expresses an optimistic state of mind. Research has shown clear links between optimism and success in learning as well as success in life.[4] Learned helplessness is a pessimistic state of mind in which failure is expected. When failure occurs it becomes a self-fulfilling prophecy which reinforces the sense of helplessness. Some of the characteristics of mastery orientation and learned helplessness are shown in Table 9.1.

The style of 'helpless' or 'mastery' oriented behaviour is not related to intelligence, but is rather a personality characteristic, a way of viewing oneself and one's capacity to be effective with people and circumstances. All individuals, whether children or adults, fall somewhere along the continuum between 'helplessness' and 'mastery'. Some children have developed the characteristics of mastery orientation or of learned help-lessness by the time they first enter school. Researchers in school entry (reception) classes, observing 4 and 5 year olds, have noted that some children show more mastery orientation than others.[5] They observed, for example:

- *reactions to difficulty* – some children avoid challenge and give up easily, whereas mastery-oriented children persist in the face of obstacles
- *independence* – mastery-oriented children show themselves to be more independent and less reliant on teacher guidance
- *attitude to learning* – mastery-oriented children are not afraid of new, challenging experiences, for example choosing learning activities such as reading books during times of free choice.

Table 9.1 Mastery orientation and learned helplessness

Mastery orientation	Learned helplessness
Willingness to try hard tasks	Unwilling to face challenges
Views problems as challenges	Views problems as 'tests' of ability
Accepts failure without excuses	Quick to offer excuses for failure
Flexible in approach, tries other ways	Rigid in approach, gives up easily
Engages in self-monitoring	Rarely engages in self-monitoring
Is self-motivated by learning	Looks for approval in learning
Wants to achieve learning goals	Wants to look good
Has a positive view of their competence	Negative view of themselves
Has a positive view of learning	Negative view of learning

By the age of 9, children can be seen to be developing either a mastery or helplessness orientation to learning. Some children have a much clearer idea about the aims of learning, and about their own capacities to learn than others. They are more aware of their own thinking processes, and whether their skills match up to the demands of a task. These abilities are developed through giving children opportunities to review what they do, to assess what they have learnt and to draw out lessons or targets for the future. It is not sufficient that children have the self-confidence to tackle intellectually demanding tasks, they also need some objective diagnosis of strengths and weaknesses in order to pursue goals successfully.

Another element in mastery orientation is the belief that intelligence can be developed. Studies show that some children believe that effort will lead to increased intelligence. 'You can become clever if you try hard', said one 6-year-old. Other children believe you can either succeed in a task or you can't, and they show little capacity for effort. As one child said, when encouraged to pursue a problem-solving task, 'It's a waste of time.' Sometimes this negative view is a result of teacher criticism, sometimes of a parental belief in 'natural talent'. As one 7 year old said, 'I'm no good at numbers, neither was my Dad. He says I'm like him.' In studies of the relatively poor performance of American children in maths, these are some of the factors cited:[6]

- insufficient time and emphasis given to academic activities
- children and parents over-estimated the children's accomplishments
- children's academic achievement was not a widely shared goal

- parents showed little involvement in children's schoolwork
- parents believed that 'natural talent' was more important in success at school than hard work.

In contrast, countries such as China and Japan, where levels of mathematics achievement measured by test scores have been shown to be higher than in the US or in Britain, one factor could be the belief of parents that intelligence is malleable, and that children can achieve educational advancement through effort. In Asian countries, there is a general view that children's effort is even more important than innate ability in determining school success. The most important legacy of this view, linked with high expectations and parental support for learning, is that these children show many of the characteristics of mastery orientation that make for success in learning.

When researcher Michael Rutter reviewed the literature on the effects of children's education on their development,[7] he concluded that:

> *The long-term educational benefits stem not from what children are specifically taught but from the effects on children's attitudes to learning, on their self-esteem, and on their task orientation.*

How can we encourage mastery-oriented children, and move them away from a sense of helplessness? How do we help children view the inevitably difficult problems they face in learning as challenges to be mastered through effort? How do we support both self-esteem and self-effort on tasks?

The following sections outline three ways in which teaching children to learn can help enhance self-esteem and mastery orientation:

- *Personalised learning* – relating learning to personal interests, thoughts and imagination, and encouraging a sense of personal responsibility and ownership of the learning process. At its best this is what 'child-centred' or 'student-centred' learning is trying to achieve. Do children understand how the topic they are learning is relevant to their lives?
- *Reviewing achievement* – identifying their areas of success and in seeing where and how they can improve by recognising, recording and reporting achievements in learning and in efforts to learn. Do children review their progress, effort and goals for the future?
- *Self-assessment* – encouraging self-regulation to increase control of the learning process, and developing insight into their thinking and learning. Do children have opportunities to assess their learning strategies and achievements?

Personalised learning

I shall only ask him, and not tell him, and he shall share the enquiry with me.
    Socrates

Personalised learning is a collaborative approach to learning in which students are encouraged to link the content of the curriculum with their own personal concerns. There are three aspects to personalised learning:

- reviewing teaching to see that it links to children's personal concerns and goals
- reviewing learning so that links are made to children's personal concerns and goals
- reviewing assessment of achievement and progress so it supports future learning.

The following example is from a lesson on fractions in maths, a subject that often fails to become linked to everyday life. At the start of the lesson, the teacher tries to personalise the topic, by helping the students appreciate how the topic of fractions is relevant to their lives. The teacher 'sells' the topic, and gets the students involved by brainstorming examples of how fractions are used in everyday life. The teacher might start by asking, 'Can you think of any examples in life where something whole is split up into parts?' Examples from one class included: dividing things into equal shares (cake, chocolate bar, etc.), sports matches (for example, 'It was a game of two halves'), TV programmes, school timetable, time, weights, measures, journeys, phases of the moon, etc.

An effective way to begin planning for teaching is to review the factual information and skills you want your children to learn. If, for example, you want to teach about another country, you might want the children to learn about:

- the map of the country
- the place of the country in relation to other countries
- places and regions within the country
- the physical environment, weather and climate
- the ways of life of the people, where they live and how they live
- the natural resources and products of the country.

A good starting point might be to write down some key personal questions you would like to have the children answer about the country. The questions aim to motivate their learning by giving them ownership of the outcomes. These questions might include:

- What do you know about the topic of study?
- What would you like to find out?

Similarly with children, a good starting point is to find out what they know, for example by asking them to write, note, map and share with others their existing knowledge. Also, ask them what they want or need to find out – what questions have they got? The following is a personal list of questions written by a 10-year-old about the proposed study of another country:

- How many people live there?
- What languages do they speak?
- Is it a clean country?
- How many different kinds of transport are there?
- Is it mainly countryside or city?
- Is it a rich or poor country?
- What is their national anthem?
- Is it full of people or not?
- Have they got a lot of endangered animals there or not?
- Do they have a good government?

LIVERPOOL JOHN MOORES UNIVERSITY
LEARNING SERVICES

The child has here a number of useful questions for research, more powerful because they are personal questions that she or he wants to find out, as well as some means for assessing at the end of the study what has been found out. What answers, after the topic of study, would the child now give to these questions? What questions have arisen during the study that she or he would like answering? How could she or he set about finding the answers? What questions have others asked? What might be the answers?

In personalising the curriculum and expecting children to take some responsibility for their own learning, we want them to relate to what they are learning, to try to involve their personal interests, thoughts and imagination. One way that has proved effective is to ask 'you-questions' that aim to help the student identify with the subject matter. 'You-questions' are addressed directly to the student. They should be relevant to personal experiences, interests and feelings and invite personal opinion, knowledge and experience. They can also be discussed and shared with others. Examples of 'you-questions' include:

- What do you know about it?
- What do you want to know?
- Have you ever been to . . . ?
- Have you ever heard about . . . ?
- What do you think it feels/felt like . . . ?

TASK 37
Reviewing personal goals
In any learning task, the students can be invited to review what they want to achieve.

Choose a topic of study and ask students to identify the task and goals (aims) of learning. Ask them also to identify the goal, intended outcome(s) and to specify criteria for success.

Figure 9.1 shows one way of recording a review of personal goals.

Assessment for learning

Reviews of research show that *assessment for learning* (AfL) can be a powerful way to improve learning, teaching and the achievement of children.[8] Assessment for learning is any assessment activity that helps to inform learners of the next steps they need to take in learning. An assessment for learning activity is successful if it informs the learner where they are, where they need to go and how to get there. It is assessment that aims to improve learning rather than just grade the learner.

Five key factors are involved in assessment for learning:

- recognising the profound effects assessment has on motivation and self-esteem
- involving children in thinking about and discussing their learning
- providing effective feedback in reviewing achievements
- helping learners to identify the next steps and set personal targets
- developing the ability to assess and understand their needs as learners.

Carol, aged 10, complained 'I know what I have to learn, I just don't know where to start.' Assessment for learning is not just about setting targets that focus on what children need to learn, but about what teachers and learners need to do next.

Topic:	
Task	*What is the task?*
Goal	*What am I trying to achieve?*
Outcome	*What am I going to do?*
Criteria	*How will I know if I am successful?*

Figure 9.1 A review of personal goals

Reviewing achievement

What is an 'achievement' in learning? A group of children brainstormed their own definitions and came up with the following list.

An achievement is something:

- you can be really proud of
- you have never done before
- which you kept on trying and finally succeeded
- you have done which you found difficult
- you have worked hard to finish
- you have done what teachers tell you is good.

We thrive under the sun of praise. We want to know what is special about us, what is praiseworthy. But we want the praise to be genuine, and to be specific to us. Children need help in identifying their areas of success and in seeing where and how they can improve in the future. Questions that can help in this process include:

- What have you learnt? *Assessing learning.*
- What have you achieved? *Assessing achievement.*

- What do you feel good about/proud of? *Assessing positive feelings.*
- What do you like doing/learning? *Assessing preferences.*
- What do you do well? *Assessing strengths.*
- What do you find hard? *Assessing difficulties and problems.*
- What don't you know/understand? *Assessing obstacles to learning.*
- What do you want to be able to do/improve/learn? *Assessing targets and plans for the future.*
- What support would help? *Assessing the need for support.*
- What do you think of yourself as a learner? *Assessing self-esteem as a learner* (a key question – see page 122).

Many teachers see the value of setting aside a particular time to talk through what children are learning and have learnt. It is a review time, a learning conversation, a conference, a time to appraise and assess how the child is doing, to recognise achievements, to establish their needs and give a sense that these needs are understood, and to discuss the next steps in learning by agreeing and setting targets. The aim is to build self-esteem by developing children's confidence in themselves as learners and giving them an increasing sense of control over the learning process so that they can become more independent learners.

Finding sufficient time in which to carry out learning conversations and reviews with individual children is a major problem for many teachers. Teachers need to give time to pupils for them to reflect on themselves as learners, their strengths and areas to develop. Most find it necessary to adopt a planned approach to managing review time. Ways this can be achieved include:

- *daily reviews* – setting aside 5 or 10 minutes at the same time each day, for example after lunch, for a review session with one or two children
- *weekly reviews* – setting aside a longer session each week, for example one afternoon, to review progress with a group of children
- *termly reviews* – setting aside a period once a term to interview each child about their progress and achievements, possibly linked to a parents' meeting
- *annual reviews* – setting aside some time for each child to discuss the work of the year and to set targets for the coming holiday/year.

In review sessions with children, the aim is to help them become better learners. Be positive about what the child can do. Keep in mind a wide range of achievements. Achievements can be in the field of personal and social endeavour, for example taking responsibility for an aspect of work or activity, being able to work constructively with others, showing persistence when work is difficult and participating in a wide range of activities. Achievements in school include evidence of progress in curriculum areas, new developments in knowledge and skill and participation in extra-curricular activities. Out-of-school achievements include the development of interests and pursuits (hobbies, collections, computer, etc.), membership of clubs and organisations, social and cultural achievements (such as languages spoken) and special skills in music, sport, etc. Remember that taking part, if it involves effort, is also an achievement.

Review
Record of a review between --. (child) and   -- (teacher) on --------------------- (date)

Achievements
What things are you pleased about?
What have you done well?
What have you worked hard on and improved?
Who or what has helped you?

Agreed targets
What are your targets for the future?
What do you want to try to improve?
How will you try to improve?
What help will you need?
Signed ---------------------------- (teacher) ---------------------------- (child)

Figure 9.2 A review record

In carrying out a review with a child, try to move from 'what' questions, such as 'What do you think your best piece of work was?', to the much harder 'why' questions, such as 'Why do you think your maths has improved?' The review should be more than a question-and-answer session, but should encourage children to speak freely and honestly about their learning experiences, and to discuss specific samples of work. As children begin to reflect on what they have done, and what has helped them, this gives the opportunity to reflect on what they could or should do in the future and what will help them achieve these goals.

Sometimes it is helpful with older children to keep a record of the review, to formalise the recording of achievements and the setting of targets. Figure 9.2 gives an example of one way of recording a review.

Target setting

One aspect of personalised learning is feedforward, helping the child to set the scene and identify future targets for learning. Another aspect is feedback, helping the child to realise what she or he has learned and has achieved. The process is a continuum, and reflects 'time future contained in time past' (Eliot). Looking back helps us to look forward. To plan for the future, we need to build on what we know of the past. To know where we are going, we need to know where we have been. We need to set targets, build on achievements, and set further targets for achievement. Targets are more likely to be met if they are agreed by us and are personal to us. As Josh, aged 11, said, 'The targets that are set for everybody are not my targets. They are only my targets if I think them for myself.'

A teacher commented:

> *Targets are very hard to keep fresh in the children's minds and achieve a 'target fresh' environment. I have them up on the wall at a height where the children can tick if they think they have achieved. We then review them as a community of enquiry once every half term.*

The best targets are those we set for ourselves and put in our own words. They provide an internal point of reference and are part of the process of self-assessment which lies at the heart of assessment for learning.

Self-assessment

One of the aims of this process is to help children move from an external point of reference to an internal point of reference. For example, when one 7 year old was asked about her reading, during a review time with her teacher, she replied, 'I think I'm good at reading because you know yesterday when I was reading with Mum she said "Well done".' However another child had some criteria by which to assess her reading, 'I have improved because last year I couldn't have read a book like Roald Dahl's *Witches*. I still don't know all the words but I can follow the story. I just guess them when I get stuck.'

TASK 38

Reviewing achievements: my school report

1 Ask your children to design a school report, for example leaving spaces for subject title, comment and grade (or mark) like this:

Name: _____	Date: _____	
Subject	Comment	Mark

2 Ask the children to use their school report to make brief comments and award themselves grades in each area of the curriculum.

3 Use the report as a basis for discussion about how the child sees their own progress in learning.

The aim of these discussions is to make achievement the focus, and to keep in mind a wide range of achievements. Remember that taking part can be an achievement, for example being a participant in learning experiences, events and activities. Self-assessments are useful for helping children discover not only what they are good at, but also to help them identify areas of weakness so that they can begin to think about ways to improve. Sometimes writing about yourself is easier than talking about yourself. One way of structuring a child's assessment of themselves is to give them statements to complete. A simple format for encouraging children's response to a task or area of learning is to ask the child to complete these four statements relating to a chosen subject or area of study, and to say why they made that assessment:

● My best piece of work was . . .
● The work I most enjoyed was . . .
● What I found most difficult was . . .
● In the future I'd like to . . .
  (or My targets for the future/ next term/next year are . . .)

Tell them you want to know what they think and why they think it.

You may wish to encourage the child to make a fuller assessment of themselves as thinkers or learners. One way of doing this is to devise a questionnaire that asks a child to respond to a range of aspects of his or her learning, for example the Self-Concept as a Thinker Scale (Figure 9.3).

Another aspect of student assessment is evaluation of the teaching they receive. What did they think of the lesson? What did they learn in the lesson? What do they still need to learn? Asking children to review what they learnt can be instructive for the teacher as well as for the students. Children are able to assess, in a subjective way but informed by a long experience of teachers and teaching, any lesson or series of lessons. This review can take the form of a scale, a written or spoken review. Lessons can be given a numerical mark, such as a percentage, or judged against an agreed scale.

Review time needs to be planned. Some teachers prefer to leave time at the end of each lesson or session, others choose a weekly review time. What is important is that criteria are discussed. What makes for a good lesson? What would help them to learn more? What should they learn next? The following task offers the opportunity for a child to give rapid feedback on any learning experience.

TASK 39

Assessing what we know

After a lesson or period of study ask students to assess:

1 What they know (or understand).
2 What they think they know.
3 What confuses them about the topic of study.

One way of recording this is to use three columns for their responses, for example:

Know or understand ✓	Think they know or understand ?	Do not understand (confused by) ✗

Self-concept as a Thinker Scale

	Never True	Rarely True	Mostly True	Always True
1 I am good at thinking	....	....	....	....
2 I am lazy at thinking	....	....	....	....
3 I am good at saying what I think	....	....	....	....
4 I am good at thinking about many things	....	....	....	....
5 I often run out of ideas	....	....	....	....
6 I am good at thinking of new ideas	....	....	....	....
7 I like thinking about difficult problems	....	....	....	....
8 I find it hard to think in real ife	....	....	....	....
9 I find it hard to concentrate	....	....	....	....
10 I am good at telling people my ideas	....	....	....	....
11 I get easily confused in my thinking	....	....	....	....
12 I usually know how to tackle a problem	....	....	....	....
13 I am good at asking questions	....	....	....	....
14 I think before deciding what is right	....	....	....	....
15 Other people listen to my ideas	....	....	....	....
16 Other people understand my ideas	....	....	....	....
17 I think about my thinking	....	....	....	....
18 I am not as good at thinking as my friends	....	....	....	....
19 I find it hard to remember	....	....	....	....
20 I am good at making plans	....	....	....	....
21 I don't think before I act	....	....	....	....
22 I am good at thinking things through	....	....	....	....
23 I find it hard to make decisions	....	....	....	....
24 I can work things out for myself	....	....	....	....

Figure 9.3 Self-concept questionnaire

One quick method of lesson review is the thumbs up (positive) or down (negative) or hand wavering (if not sure). Sometimes the 'not sures' are the most productive to question as this can confirm their learning or confusions and help clarify learning for others.

A useful strategy for encouraging the articulation of doubts, problems, confusions and uncertainties is to have a problem box in which students may put in 'help slips'. In one class when the children were asked to review the usefulness of their problem box, they wrote:

- It's a good way to get messages to the teacher.
- When we get stuck, it means it can get sorted out.
- Sometimes you need help but do not know how to ask for it. Now we can use the problem box.

Problems can be tackled by the teacher or shared with the whole class. The message of the problem box is that we all have problems – it helps to say what your problems are and that they can be solved if you ask for help.

Self-awareness

Children can also be helped to gain self-awareness through thinking about what goes on in their minds or brains when they think and learn. The aim is to help them to become more self-aware, more conscious of their mental processes and to show them that they have some control over the way their brains work – some self-mastery. The following are some reflective comments by children on how they would describe the workings of their brains:

> *My brain is like a massive forest. It's full of amazing ideas. But some of these ideas are like shy animals, they hide away in the middle of the forest. I don't think we can ever really understand how our brains work.*

> *My brain is like an anthill, with millions of tiny passageways. There is always something going on in my head. The ants in my mind never seem to rest. I just hope there aren't any ant-eaters!*

> *My brain is like a naughty puppy. It never seems to do what I want it to. If I've got maths homework to do, it wants to read a comic or watch TV. But like a puppy it can be trained.*

Children can also be encouraged to draw the workings of their brains and minds.[9] Drawing is one way of organising thinking, other ways are through organised talking (see Chapter 4) and thinking through writing. Writing has a key role to play in facilitating thinking and learning in all subjects. There has been much research into ways of developing the link between thinking and writing.[10]

Many teachers encourage their students to keep journals, learning logs or 'think books' as intellectual diaries in which to record their questions, observations and feelings about what has been taught, as a form of continuing review of the learning process. What arises from research into the use of student journals is that children need help in keeping and learning from their journals. One way of helping children is to make the journal interactive, with the teacher or a chosen response partner making a written response to journal entries. Some teachers prefer to make the journals private, so that children can feel free to record their true feelings and observations – like a writer's journal. Expressing their own observations and knowledge in their own words helps them to know and understand more about what they have learnt and about themselves as learners.

Figure 9.4 is an example of a child thinking through writing, about the process of writing.[11]

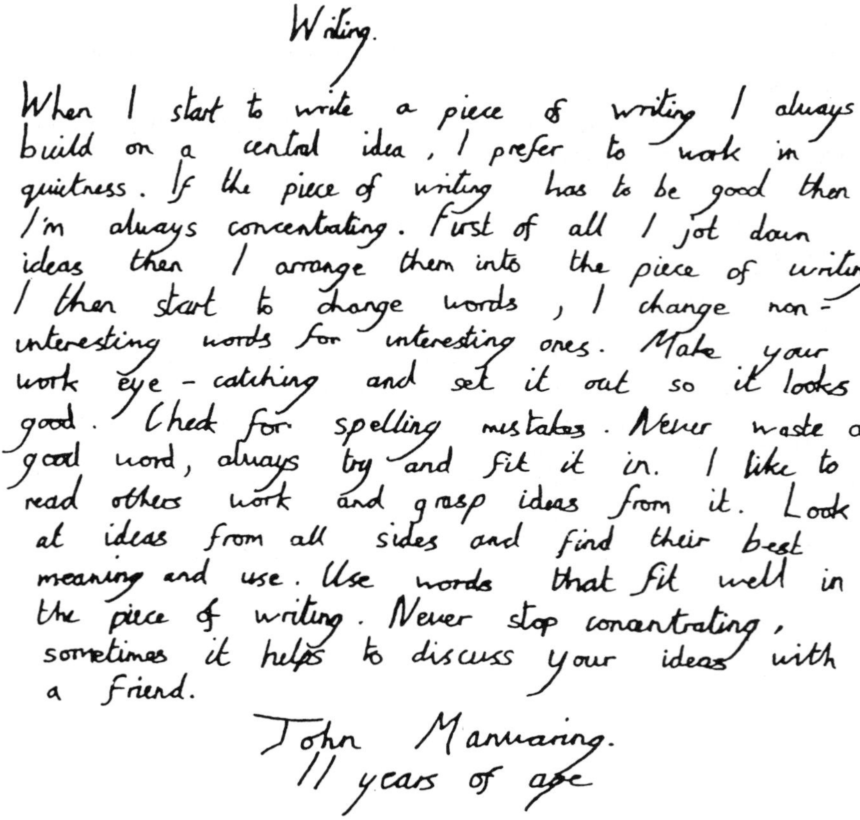

> Writing.
>
> When I start to write a piece of writing I always build on a central idea, I prefer to work in quietness. If the piece of writing has to be good then I'm always concentrating. First of all I jot down ideas then I arrange them into the piece of writing. I then start to change words, I change non-interesting words for interesting ones. Make your work eye-catching and set it out so it looks good. Check for spelling mistakes. Never waste a good word, always try and fit it in. I like to read others work and grasp ideas from it. Look at ideas from all sides and find their best meaning and use. Use words that fit well in the piece of writing. Never stop concentrating, sometimes it helps to discuss your ideas with a friend.
>
> John Manwaring.
> 11 years of age

Figure 9.4 'Writing', by John Manwaring aged 11

Every child needs a personal tutor, or mediator of their learning experience, who can facilitate the processes of review and reflection. The following are some of the principles of mediated learning which Feuerstein and his team of researchers[12] have identified as essential to children's learning. The process of review is an ideal means for developing these important metacognitive functions which are the tools of independent learning:

- *inner meaning* – having a sense of purpose about learning, knowing the reasons for, and the value and significance of learning activities
- *self-regulation* – developing the need to think about and plan their work, encouraging self-control and personal responsibility in learning
- *feelings of competence* – feeling confident about learning, knowing what you can do and how to get help

- *feelings of challenge* – being self-aware, knowing how to deal with challenge and difficulty
- *communicating* – developing the ability to communicate, to share thoughts through discussion, writing and creative expression
- *setting targets* – setting your personal goals or objectives to aim for, having high but realistic expectations
- *being aware of self-change* – knowing that you can change, gaining feedback on learning and identifying achievements.

Summary

In helping children to review their learning, we can develop in them a more confident sense of themselves and increase their awareness of themselves and of the learning process. This means finding ways to develop self-esteem and a sense of mastery in learning. This can be developed through personalised learning which focuses on the needs of the learner, through recognising achievement and setting targets for learning, and through developing the skills of self-assessment. The skills of self-assessment can help the student develop self-awareness and many of the metacognitive tools of independent learning.

LIVERPOOL
JOHN MOORES UNIVERSITY
I.M MARSH LRC
Tel: 0151 231 5216

10 Creating powerful learning environments

Ways to create effective communities for learning

A good school does not emerge like a pre-packed frozen dinner stuck for 15 seconds in a radar range; it develops from the slow simmering of carefully blended ingredients.
Ted Sizer

I learn best when I'm with other people, sometimes this is in school, sometimes it isn't.
Fatima, aged 12

In a tough inner city school in London, a teacher has a class of low-achieving children, many of whom are from socially and economically deprived backgrounds. She is keen to raise a sense of self-esteem and expectations of achievement in her children. She calls them all 'Smarties' and says they are smart and sweet, smart of mind and sweet of nature (they are also of many different colours). By affirming they are smart, not once but repeatedly, she hopes they will come to believe it. She tries to 'catch them being good', good at their work and good in their response to others. She encourages them to make affirmations about each other – 'John, tell us who you think has been working well in your group', 'Selina, pick out someone who has been helpful to you today', 'Ricky, can you find two good things to say about Sophie's story?'

What are the characteristics of a community that supports the success and achievements of individuals within it? One of the characteristics is 'high cohesion', which is the sense of 'belonging', of shared purpose and support within a group. The strength of a high-cohesion group is that it has a strong identity. Examples of this might include a high-cohesion society (like Japan), a high-cohesion school (like Eton) or a successful sports team (like the All Blacks). A potential disadvantage of high-cohesive groups is that individual growth can become subservient to group norms, as anyone who has experienced the stifling influence of village life or a very close-knit family may experience. The ideal is to belong to a high-cohesion group which supports the growth of each individual. The following are some elements that can support an ethos of success in learning for the group and for the individuals within it. A positive climate evolves out of:

- *loyalty* – nurturing a sense of belonging to a community, showing loyalty to individuals within it, and communicating confidence in their ability to think and learn
- *trust* – involving members in decision-making, and giving each some responsibility in negotiating the outcomes of learning
- *support* – offering help and encouragement in learning, being committed to the growth and learning of individuals
- *dynamism* – showing energy and enthusiasm in the pursuit of goals, sustaining morale when faced with the challenges of learning

- *expectation* – setting goals, being clear about assumptions, beliefs and learning outcomes
- *communication* – sharing information about success and failure, creating a common bond of shared knowledge.

All successful supportive communities share some or all of the above characteristics. In good schools, these evolve over time, and are the fruit of the sustained vision of the head and teachers within the school. Thus, the traditions or cultural values of the school are built up and provide a continuity of purpose through times of change and challenge. The school is made up of smaller learning communities, such as individual classes, and these can provide powerful environments for learning. What makes a learning environment powerful is when the whole community – students, teachers and other adults – agrees on what they believe about learning and supports those beliefs with action.

Creating a learning community in the classroom

In a sense, a supportive group is like a tribe. The themes of identity, support and community – the sense of 'belonging' inherent and admired in traditional tribal societies – can help create a powerful environment for learning.

One successful programme for building supportive communities in the school or classroom is called 'Tribes'.[1] The Tribes programme organises a class into groups of five or six children who work together throughout the school year. The children can name friends they wish to have in their tribes, but each tribe must have a mixture of boys and girls and be of mixed ability. The aim is to develop in each group positive peer regard so that it will create a supportive climate for learning that will help enhance self-image, positive behaviour and academic achievement.

There are certain ground rules that students are expected to honour at all times within their groups. Among the behaviours that are expected to become the norms of the group are:

- *attentive listening* – paying close attention to one another's words and feelings, giving care, respect and consideration
- *no put-downs* – appreciating others, making helpful contributions and avoiding negative remarks, name calling, hurtful gestures or behaviour
- *right to pass* – choosing when to participate in group discussion and activity, having the right to silence within a group setting
- *confidentiality* – honouring the group's sharing, being confident that 'what we say here stays here'.

These rules, or similar ones agreed by the groups and expressed in their words, are posted in a prominent place in the classroom. What makes the Tribes process unique is the establishment of long-term support groups within the classroom, rather than the random and changing groupings found in many classrooms. It emphasises the need to get the setting for learning right and that an intentionally created support system will help create a more dynamic and supportive environment for learning. It stresses the importance of teacher and peer role modelling to teach interpersonal skills and caring behaviour. In focusing on children's social development, it aims also to enhance academic achievement and the ability to learn.

One of the key aims of creating a learning community should be to foster a sense of inclusion in the group and in any group endeavour – to help children feel included and of value. We want them included in the community of thinkers and learners. This means that three basic opportunities should be provided within any group setting or learning environment:

- *introduction* – each member needs to introduce himself or herself not just by name but by being given the chance to describe his or her interests and experiences
- *self-expression* – each person should be able to express what she or he hopes and expects from the group's time together, a chance to be part of setting the agenda
- *acknowledgement* – each person needs to be acknowledged as having been heard and appreciated.

All learners feel, at times, vulnerable and defensive. Time spent on building a sense of inclusion and trust is time well spent. Learning is not easy to achieve at times of emotional disturbance or social disruption. If emotional needs are ignored, the energy of the learner is deflected away from his or her capacity to accomplish learning tasks. In helping children to state their feelings clearly, or to discuss and reflect on situations of concern, we are helping them to learn about themselves and about other people. If we can utilise the co-operative spirit of the group to address problems and support individuals, we are creating powerful allies in the process of creating renewed energy for learning.

Circle time

An activity central to approaches which aim to build a community (see also community of enquiry, page 54) is 'circle time'. The usual format for this is to sit in a circle, with the teacher as part of the circle, and leading the group in a sharing activity. Experience in the large group provides an opportunity to model the norms we hope the child will follow in other, smaller learning groups. The virtue of a circle is that everyone can see the face of every other member – and can talk person to person with any other member.

It is important that the teacher models the norms she or he hopes the children will learn, and in particular that most difficult of skills – attentive listening. Attentive listening means acknowledging the speaker, giving full attention and eye contact. It means that attention is given not only to the words that are spoken, but also to the feelings behind the words. As one child put it; 'What you feel is part of what you say.' We all find it easy to pretend to listen, but there are tell-tale signs. We can see in the eyes of others when they are not attending, when their thoughts are elsewhere, when the shutters are open but no one is at home.

Some of the active listening skills that we should practise include:

- *attending* – listening silently with full attention
- *encouraging* – encouragement through non-verbal (nodding) or verbal ('uh huh') means
- *paraphrasing* – 'what I heard you say was . . .'
- *responding* – responding to the words, and reflecting feelings ('you sound sad').

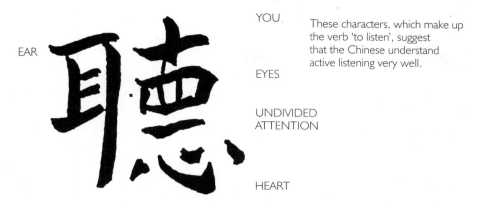

EAR   YOU   These characters, which make up the verb 'to listen', suggest that the Chinese understand active listening very well.

EYES

UNDIVIDED ATTENTION

HEART

Figure 10.1 Chinese character: 'to listen'

A book written many years ago with the title *The Geranium on the Windowsill Just Died, but Teacher, You Went Right On* was about a teacher who refused to acknowledge anything not in her lesson plan. She did not allow time for children to talk about anything not on her agenda. There was no time to mourn the geranium. Many seemingly small events can be enormously important for a child – losing a tooth, falling out with a friend, not understanding what others are doing. In allowing time to report, reflect and discuss we are showing that learning is about life and what is important in life. The concerns of the learner are equally as important as the concerns of the teacher, and we need to find out what these are.

One way to check on children before they start a learning activity is to provide opportunities for comment, for example by asking, 'Is there anything anyone wants to say before we start?', 'Are there any problems?' A problem shared is not always a problem halved, but when people are involved together in finding a solution to a problem, they are more likely to find a solution and to accept responsibility for making the solution work.

In leading a group or class through a step-by-step process of problem-solving, it may be helpful to recall the teaching cycle of Romance–Precision–Generalisation advocated by Whitehead.[2]

- 'Romance' means awaking the sense of wonder and engaging the learner's imagination, for example through embodying the problem or investigation in a story.
- 'Precision' involves studying the details of the problem or issue, building deeper knowledge of the words, objects and processes – the inductive phase.
- 'Generalisation' is how we sum up what we have learnt through new concepts, solutions, definitions, connections, applications and uses of materials and ideas.

In identifying the problem, try to get the children to identify with the problem or an aspect of the problem, to try to embed it in their own human experience by an act of imagination, by making them part of the story. The following task presents one problem and process for group problem solving.

TASK 40

Reviewing a problem

Give the group of children a problem to solve. Ask them:

1 What is the problem? Whose problem is it? Why is it a problem?
2 What are the possible solutions?
3 What are the best solutions?
4 How will we implement their solutions?
5 How will they find out if they work?

Sample problem: Bullying

Older children are reported to be bullying younger children in the playground. How will the group try to solve the problem? One step-by-step process would be:

1 Identify the problem – get group members to remember or imagine how they felt when they were young and were picked on by older children.
2 Generate solutions – brainstorm in groups ideas for bringing bullying to an end, and list them
3 Choose the best options – ask each group to select three best ideas, compile a class list of ideas, discuss and vote on the best ideas to solve the problem.
4 Implement the solutions – discuss how to translate good ideas into practice.
5 Test the solutions – what are the criteria for success? Who will judge, how and when?

A good time to reinforce the sense of community in the classroom is at the end of a learning activity. This can be done through a process of group review (see Chapter 9), asking such questions as:

- What did you/we do in this lesson? (Show and tell.)
- What have you learnt?
- What did you like about this activity?
- What didn't you like about this lesson?
- How should we continue what we've been doing?

Another strategy is 'Last words', which is to ask all the group to have a turn, if they wish, to say something about the topic that they have not had the chance of saying. During this time, no one must interrupt or respond. It is simply a time when each member has one, and only one, chance to say a few last words before the session ends.

Creating a learning community in the school

Research into creating learning environments in school is building the foundations for a systematic approach to improving the effectiveness of schools.[3] Its findings give teachers and schools clues as to what they should focus on in improving their schools and their students' chances of success. One of the keys to school effectiveness identified by Mortimore is 'intellectually challenging teaching'. There seems to be a link between effective schools and those teaching and learning strategies that focus on challenging and developing thinking.

The growing emphasis on school effectiveness and school improvement reflects general concerns about the working of organisations that have concerned managers and politicians over the last three decades.[4] This has coincided with times of tremendous change for both business organisations and schools. Studies of how effective organisations cope with change, what makes for excellence and how successful organisations relate to their customers and workforce have identified three key factors:

- the quality of planning within the organisation
- the nature of the culture within the organisation
- the ability of organisations to focus on their key functions ('sticking to the knitting').

These match well to what research has identified as the three issues central to the success of schools – development planning, school ethos and quality in teaching and learning.

Over recent years there has been a change of climate in the expectations held of schools. The growing research evidence that 'schools make a difference' has done much to dispel the pessimism of the 1960s and 1970s. Schools had for a decade or more been charged by social critics with a cultural conservatism that perpetuated and exaggerated social inequalities. Schools could not counter the effects of class and culture. Some radical critics argued that real education could only be achieved outside of the school system.

Pioneering research in the late 1970s demonstrated that some schools were more effective than others, and that there was a 'school effect' (Rutter, 1979).[4] By comparing students on entry and on leaving school they developed the concept of 'added value', which is the educational benefit to the child specifically provided by the school over a period of time.

Studies of secondary schools by Rutter identified some common characteristics in effective schools, what he called 'process characteristics', and these factors have been largely confirmed in subsequent studies in this country and abroad. These factors, in order of importance, are:

- leadership
- school climate
- pupil–teacher relationship
- quality of curriculum/teaching
- pupil socio-economic background
- evaluation
- financial resources
- physical characteristics.

Researchers found strong links between some of these features, especially between most consistent factors such as leadership and school climate, pupil–teacher relationships and learning/teaching. There has been much debate on criteria and research methods used to assess achievement, but the central question, 'Are some schools more effective than others?' has clearly been answered. Research studies have tended to find that effective schools are likely to be effective for everyone in them. Current research is now probing questions related to the complexities and differences between schools and within schools. For example are there differential effects between classes in one school, or even within the same classroom?

Researchers have begun to take an interest in 'moving schools', a term taken from business management to indicate dynamic and developing schools, as opposed to 'stuck' or declining schools. Research has supported what many teachers have found from experience – that there can be good teachers in 'stuck' or declining schools, and of 'rump' groups or departments left behind in developing schools. It is clear that effective proponents of change need to value individual differences and be sensitive to the needs of teachers in a time of change. It is also clear that the richest culture for change is one in which everyone has something to gain and where all – school leaders, teachers and pupils – are involved in learning.[5]

Improving schools

The effective school is an improving school. Disraeli once said, 'In a perfect man change is constant.' We might paraphrase this to read. 'In a perfect school change is constant.' However, it is the quality of change that is the key, and the way that change affects every individual and aspect of the school. The three key areas that relate to effectiveness and improvement are:

- school improvement planning
- ethos
- teaching and learning
- rigorous self-evaluation.

School improvement planning

School development planning is the enabling mechanism whereby schools can adopt a planned approach to change and improvement. Schools in many countries in Europe, Australia, Canada and the USA schools being required or encouraged to create a rolling programme of school development plans. The school improvement process has been likened to a journey – planning becomes the means of transport to the destination, and the plan is the map for the journey. One of the dangers is the map becoming the destination. School improvers need to beware of planning being a mere pen-and-paper exercise.

Improvements within the classroom depend on improvements outside the classroom. School development planning must focus on 'the total school', so that all elements that are important to teachers, governors, parents and pupils are included. Important elements of development planning include:

- *process* – the focus of planning, the planning team, the planning programme
- *ownership* – the widest participation and collaboration in the process, negotiated outcomes
- *evaluation* – agreement on what, why and how the plan is to be monitored and assessed.

Two questions that can be asked about any plan are:

- Does the plan support the aims and ethos of the school?
- Does the plan result in improvements in learning, teaching and attainment of pupils?

School ethos

One consistent finding of research into effective schools is that 'ethos' is an important ingredient. Ethos is defined as the climate of the school, and is expressed in the organisational conditions and web of personal relationships within the school. Ethos and school culture are difficult to define. They are the outward expression of the 'secret harmonies' of the school, those norms, beliefs and values that become modes, standards and rules of operation. As one inspector put it, 'It's what you feel in your bones about a school when you have been in it for sometime.' It is clear from research that there is something intangible about a school, a style, tone and atmosphere that effects pupil performance. An effective school has a positive ethos, reflected in a range of factors which include:

- *a sense of identity and pride in the school* – good schools have a sense of cohesion
- *a welcoming environment* – good schools present themselves in positive ways
- *high pupil and teacher expectations* – good schools expect the best of people
- *strong and purposeful leadership* – good schools are well managed
- *positive attitudes towards pupils* – good schools motivate through praise
- *work in partnership with parents and the community* – good schools involve others.

One way schools can identify actions needed to enhance their ethos is to conduct an ethos survey – to ask pupils, teachers and parents what they think of the school and how it could be improved. Examples of ways to improve school ethos might include developing opportunities for extra-curricular activities, encouraging parents and members of the community to involve themselves in school activities or provide reward systems in which all pupils can benefit. Indicators of success in developing school ethos might include pupil achievement in academic and non-academic pursuits, better attendance, more time on task in the classroom, more investment in homework, and perceptions of better pupil–teacher relationships.

Improving learning and teaching

A good school is said to be 'learner centred', 'learning enriched' and a 'learning community', one in which adults as well as students are engaged in lifelong learning, dedicated to the growth of individuals and the realisation of human potential. Research, however, highlights a tension between the needs of the individual as learner and the job of the teacher to cater for the many and simultaneous dimensions of learning in the classroom. In looking at improving teaching and learning, we need to look at what teachers do and what learners do, and the critical relationship between the two.

Research highlights the differences in learning style and developmental needs of students. Classroom teachers and school policies will seek to maximise learning opportunities for individuals in different ways, for example by providing opportunities for:

- *independent learning* – where the pupil's relationship is primarily with learning resources
- *supported learning* – where the relationship is primarily between learner and teacher
- *peer learning* – where there is a learning/teaching relationship between pupils in pairs and groups
- *extended learning* – supported learning out of school, including homework and home study.

We know that effective teachers exhibit an impressive range of competencies, including *curriculum knowledge* (the content of teaching), *pedagogical knowledge* (the skills of teaching in theory and application, which include the skills of presentation, organisation and management of learning), *psychological knowledge* of children as individuals and *sociological knowledge* of the nature of cultural and social groups. In addition, they need *evaluative skills* to assess children's learning and the effectiveness of their own teaching. Effective teaching is a complex activity that needs not only the professional skills mentioned, but also personal qualities such as imagination, creativity and sensitivity to stimulate, support and encourage learning. But we know that even this list is not sufficient to guarantee learning. Determined pupils can and do resist even the most skilled of teachers. Learning can also take place in the absence of effective teaching. However best results are likely to occur when there is a match between effective teaching and learning.

How can we tell when there is effective teaching and learning? The following are some indicators:

- *Student outcomes*
    - achievement – evidence of progress and achievement
    - ethos – general attitudes to school and learning
    - self-concept – measures of self-concept and motivation as learners
    - behaviour – measures of improved behaviour
    - attendance – good attendance/truancy measures
    - further education – measures of post-school progress.
- *Teacher/school outcomes*
    - ethos – survey of attitudes to school/teaching
    - professional development – survey of teacher as learner/extended professional study
    - staff absence
    - quality of teaching – student outcomes and relationships
    - assessment – monitoring student progress and self-evaluation.

A key lesson from school effectiveness research is that ends – outcomes in terms of effective teaching and learning – must always be kept in sight. Schools must always keep in sight their primary purpose, and whilst keeping a keen eye on the internal challenge both to maintain what is good and to strive for the better, they should also look at the example of other successful schools.

Effective schools – places where children succeed

Effective schools are places where children succeed. Questions arise of course. What constitutes success? How can successful schools be identified? How can you compare schools serving different communities? In one study,[6] schools were identified against various criteria of quality. The schools identified came from a variety of social settings, and the conclusions turn out to be surprisingly similar to other studies researching into school effectiveness, such as Peter Mortimore's junior school project. From this research, two lessons are clear:

- Excellence can be achieved anywhere – in urban, suburban and rural schools, in schools of varied size (from 40 to over 1000 pupils), in both streamed and unstreamed schools.
- Themes that work are within the reach of all schools.

Research into effective schools identifies as indicators of quality and effectiveness the following ten elements:[7]

- teaching that develops competence and character
- setting high expectations, monitoring standards and rewarding results
- school leadership
- clear goals and core values
- creating professional work environments
- positive student–teacher relationships
- resources to facilitate teaching and learning
- working in the community
- solving problems
- being unique.

Teaching that develops competence and character

Good schools combine effective teaching (clear goals, a broad but rigorous curriculum and capable committed teachers) with successful socialisation of students (characterised by positive behaviour, good work habits and a commitment to the school community). Teachers had clearly focused views on the needs of their children. The most frequently mentioned needs were:

- basic skills – 87 per cent
- higher order thinking skills – 32 per cent
- self-esteem and personal development – 31 per cent
- good citizenship/preparation for adult life – 31 per cent.

In effective schools, resources and programmes vary. What is common is teachers who work hard to provide active and intellectually-challenging teaching in a warm, supportive environment.

Setting high expectations, monitoring standards and rewarding results

Good teachers and good schools set and communicate high expectations of academic performance and behaviour. Successful schools believe that all pupils can be motivated to learn. They are characterised by intensive care and strong reward or recognition systems. They make increased demands on their pupils, but they balance this with increased recognition for success, for example in formal year achievement assemblies, and informal use of congratulatory messages to pupils and parents.

To be maintained, these standards must be monitored and reinforced by appropriate rewards. The dilemma is that you cannot hold uniformly high expectations of all students. Good teachers work to overcome this by maintaining high standards for their classes over the long term, while in the short term varying their expectations for individual students, motivating their best work and recognising their achievements.

School leadership

Effective leadership is essential for school success. Dynamic leadership often stems from the head, but to be truly effective must be distributed amongst other leaders of learning inside and beyond the school. Research about the most effective leaders shows that they use a range of styles including:[8]

- *coercive* – do it now in this way.
- *authoritative* – let me tell you about where we're going as a school and why.
- *affiliative* – the most important thing is that we get on with each other.
- *democratic* – we will make decisions together.
- *pacesetting* – watch me do it – I'm setting the standard.
- *coaching* – let's explore what happened and identify what we can do differently next time.

There is no one style or formula for effective leadership except in the sense that the best leaders are learning centred – they focus on the needs of learners and select the appropriate leadership style to match the leadership challenge. The best leaders adapt to their local school context. They:

- set and maintain a clear direction, articulating a shared vision/mission for the school
- support their teams with policies, programmes and professional development
- concentrate on changes most likely to lead to improvement.

There is not just one leader. Leadership in good schools is distributed and shared. Good leaders develop other leaders and create leadership teams where many individuals take leadership roles. Good leaders link strong monitoring control, with collective responsibility and a maximising of individual autonomy (similarly good teachers do this in the classroom).

Clear goals and core values

A shared purpose is achieved by agreeing common goals. These are given clarity by being written down and shared with all in the community – teachers, students, parents and local community. School success comes from vision linked to action. The shared purposes must be taken seriously and translated into action. Such a vision can form the basis for decisive action and the creation of a shared moral order. Establishing priorities will help to give them clear identity and can strengthen loyalty.

Creating professional work environments

Good schools share a collective sense of control. Individuals do not feel isolated – there is a sense of community, a satisfaction from being part of the group and school. This is achieved by maintaining the right balance of control and freedom. Seven elements are identified in the research as contributing to developing good people and a good environment:[9]

- a sense of belonging
- a respect for teaching and for teachers
- a sense of control over the job
- support for personal and professional development
- care for the physical condition of the school

- recognition for effort
- reward for achievement.

Effective schools aim to raise the professional status of their teachers. They do this by increasing teachers' decision-making responsibilities and by creating good working conditions. This, in turn, is reflected in high staff attendance and low staff turnover. A sense of community and common purpose is fostered by making group involvement a priority in decision making, building in planning time and in showing appreciation of good work.

Positive student–teacher relationships

Successful schools and classes are characterised by students who try harder and show greater effort. They are well motivated. How is this achieved? Students are motivated through formal and informal relationships. In many of these schools, teachers and students are given opportunities to meet informally, for example through extra-curricular activities, or through use of libraries, computer centres or other facilities in their free time, or in time when they can seek out a teacher for personal assistance. In some schools, each department has a work/resource centre open to students outside class time. In others, all students have a personal tutor who follows their career (about 10–15 students per tutor) and supports their progress through school. Good schools tend to work on being caring schools. One way they do this is to use their resources to provide lower pupil:teacher ratios, more pupil–teacher contact.

Resources to facilitate teaching and learning

Adequate resources, and the use of resources for the maximum effect, can make a big difference to a school. Vital resources include:

- *time* – maximum use should be made of classroom learning time, with few interruptions, non-teaching activity reduced to a minimum, and time on learning tasks maximised
- *space* – good schools and teachers try to use every available space for learning purposes
- *voluntary help* – good schools have active voluntary help programmes to support teaching and learning.

Working in the community

Good schools are characterised by high degrees of parental and community involvement. Two keys to community links are:

- *a broad definition of community* to include neighbours, local businesses, other service organisations, senior citizens and any others willing to help the school and its children
- *strong communication links* including home–school links, pre- and post-school links, with regular letters from staff summarising goals/achievements, previewing studies and informing news and needs. These links are pursued with energy, sincerity and seriousness, and are seen not as window-dressing but as a critical element in school success.

Elements of working with the community include human resources such as voluntary help in clerical duties, to teach, tutor, help with, plan and implement activities. Many schools have active volunteer programmes such as a 'grandpeople programme' for non-parents and the retired to help with groups or with specific subject skills, or as consultants. Public relations helps develop community links through strong PTAs, informative newsletters, sponsorship and fundraising. Community service is shown by the way the school invite themselves into the community to share and to serve. These and other ways help to build the identity of the school and affirm its core values.

Solving problems

A characteristic of all schools, including the most successful ones, is that they have problems – obstacles to success. These may include inadequate facilities, inadequate funding, poor discipline, low attendance, falling rolls, complacency, drug abuse, low standards, poor school spirit, poor community relations, and so on. Successful schools try to identify their problems and search aggressively for solutions, for example in short 'target sessions' 15 minutes before school to discuss a 'problem' student. They tend to be solution focused rather than problem focused.

The path to excellence is strewn with obstacles. There is an underlying need for stubbornness and commitment in the face of problems, an unwillingness to accept defeat or mediocrity, not settling for 'good enough' but seeking to do better. This involves not just talking about action, but a 'can do' philosophy showing itself in a willingness to do some positive problem-solving.

Being unique

Excellent schools, like excellent teachers, are all different. Each has its own unique characteristics. Indeed they often strive to achieve uniqueness. They express their uniqueness by:

- being innovative and open to change while holding fast to the core of their vision and values
- being responsive to those whom they serve
- valuing what is special about their learning community
- having a bias for action, for getting on with the job – but they like to do it in their own way, having the capacity to renew vitality and performance.
- using informed opportunism to allow for a flexibility in planning, to make the most of 'happy accidents'
- being committed to teaching and to the peculiarities of their school and of the team working within it.

TASK 41

Creating goals

Questions to ask in seeking to create a powerful learning environment include:
- What goals or outcomes do you want for your students?
- How are they communicated?
- Who knows them?
- When are they reviewed?

Identify the characteristics of the learning environment which you wish to create. List these characteristics in order of importance.

The evidence of the research summarised above shows that successful schools do not necessarily have new approaches. What they do have are high levels of awareness of, and participation in, strategies that are tried and tested and that work. It is an incomplete picture with many pieces missing, but the themes here reflect the general conclusions arising from research literature. Specific policies and practices may be less important than the standards accepted by teachers and students and the general 'ethos' that unites them into a caring community. From a working consensus about the purpose of education comes a clarity of intent, and from this all else (including a sense of pride and commitment) can follow. Research shows that there is no single or simple answer, no one solution or magic formula. Success comes from the chemistry of all the small positive things that count, blended by the uniqueness of the teacher and school in different ways to create places where children succeed.

Transforming the learning community

I feel part of this school, because they ask me what I think and I think how things could be better.

Lee, aged 10

A school seeking to achieve its goals is in a process of continual change. Processes that help in the continual development of a learning community include:

- consultation with pupils
- extension into the community
- networking through ICT
- investment in good teaching and care.

Consultation

Children benefit from being asked what they think about their teacher and their learning environment. So how can teachers find out what it feels like to be a pupil in their class, at the receiving end of teaching? Questionnaires and pupil perception interviews are some of the ways schools are auditing the impact of classroom climate and teaching styles on pupils' learning.

One such questionnaire (produced by the Hay Group)[10] focuses questions on nine aspects of children's experience of learning and teaching in school:

- *clarity* – children are clear about their teacher's expectations for work and behaviour
- *environment* – the classroom is clean, tidy and attractive
- *fairness* – perceived absence of favouritism in terms of help and praise given
- *interest* – children feel they are learning things in an interesting way
- *order* – children pay attention, behave well and don't interfere with each other's work
- *participation* – children feel able to ask questions and offer opinions in class
- *safety* – children feel safe from emotional or physical bullying or other factors that arouse fear

- *standards* – children understand what is expected of them in terms of performance and are encouraged to improve
- *support* – children can get help when they need, they help each other and are friendly towards each other.

Many schools design their own questionnaires for pupils to find out their views on specific things, for example on writing, which subjects they like best/least and why, or behaviour. All such surveys, if analysed effectively, can add to schools' understanding of how learning and teaching are received and enable them to take stock and review current practice.

TASK 42
Consulting children about their learning environment
Design a questionnaire to find out what children think about their learning environment.
1 Identify what you think are the most important characteristics of the learning environment.
2 Turn these characteristics into questions to ask children.
3 Discuss these questions with teachers and children. Could they be improved?
4 Use the questionnaire to get feedback from children.
5 Analyse the findings from the questionnaire.
6 Discuss with children ways in which the learning environment could be improved.

School councils also provide a means for the pupils' voices to be heard and add to the inclusive nature of a school (www.schoolscouncils.org).

Extension

An extended school is one that provides a range of services and activities, often beyond the school day, to help meet the needs of its pupils, their families and the wider community. Schools need to creatively consider how they can be a centre for learning within their community. Research shows that the provision of community services in schools can improve pupil attainment, behaviour and attendance, support family involvement in children's learning and boost community pride and involvement. One report[11] showed that:

- a school providing out-of-school art-based activities saw a dramatic rise in its GCSE results in creative arts subjects
- out-of-school activities had positive impacts on motivation and attainment
- parents involved in adult education projects reported positive effects on their perceptions of themselves as learners and on their ability to act as role models for their children
- where the local community was involved in planning the extended school, community members reported a growing sense of self-esteem and of control over decisions which affected their lives.

Networking through ICT

Information and communication technology (ICT) can provide powerful tools for learning and for creating learning environments. Research[12] shows that when well used ICT can help to:

- raise pupil attainment
- increase pupil motivation and self-esteem
- improving pupil behaviour
- increase the efficiency of school administration
- develop more effective systems of assessment
- improve internal and external school communications.

The use of ICT can enable teachers and carers to introduce a greater variety of stimuli to capture children's interest, generate enthusiasm and prompt ideas and thinking. However, it is difficult to show conclusively that ICT raises attainment levels, due to the large number of other contextual factors involved in any learning situation. What it provides is improved access to different media and resources for children to explore. ICT is a tool of communication that can help in teaching, but it does not do the teaching or the learning.

At a routine level, ICT can allow administrative tasks to be carried out more quickly. It is particularly useful in the tracking and assessment of pupils, providing collection and analysis of pupil performance data. Computer programs can encourage the exercise of higher order thinking skills. Extended learning communities can be created through use of ICT, extending both internal and external communications between pupils and teachers. 'Virtual classrooms' can be used to develop self-evaluation, as virtual discussions would allow schools to listen to their pupils and parents, leading to more effective evaluation of teaching and learning. Children often identify access to computers as an important element in supporting their learning. But it is not the hardware, the cameras and computers, that guarantees learning but interaction with the human software. What comes out of consultations with children is the value they place on the people they are with – their teachers, helpers and fellow learners.

TASK 43

Developing ICT as a tool for learning and teaching

1   Consider the use of ICT in your own teaching and discuss with others:
    Where have you used ICT?
    Where was it most successful?
    Why was it successful?
    What problems did you face in use of ICT?
    What aspects of ICT did you not use and, if so, why?

2   Consider the use of ICT in your future planning and discuss with others:
    What features of ICT do you plan to use?
    How will ICT support learning and teaching?
    Are there aspects of ICT not being used and, if so, why?
    What help do you need to support your teaching with ICT?
    What new goals do you have in using ICT in your teaching?

Investment in good teaching and care

Above all, it is good teaching and care, at home, at school and in the community that is the key to children's progress in learning. There is no better investment in the future of children than providing good or excellent teaching. So what makes an excellent teacher? According to school inspectors:[13]

> *In excellent teaching difficult ideas are taught in an inspiring and highly effective way. All pupils are engrossed in their work and make considerably better progress than might be expected. Achievement is very high. Teaching is stimulating, enthusiastic and consistently challenging, stemming from expert knowledge of the curriculum, how to teach it and how pupils learn. There are excellent relationships in the classroom. Teaching methods are well selected and time is used very productively for whole-class, independent and collaborative work. Activities and demands are matched sensitively to pupils' needs. Well-directed teaching assistants reinforce and support learning very effectively.*

For David, aged 11, what a good teacher does is to help create the emotional conditions for learning to take place – or, in his words, 'a happy class' (see Figure 10.2).

My recipe for a happy class

Ingredients

1 pinch of sharing
1/2 cup of confidence
1 tbsp of enjoyment
6 tsp of cheerfulness
5 oz of communication
1/2 kg of good looks
250g co-operation
10g behaviour
1 kg of discipline
1 really nice teacher (grated)
500 ml of kindness

Method

Mix the confidence, communication and co-operation together in a large bowl.
Add the enjoyment, the cheerfulness and the good looks to the mixture.
Beat together the behaviour, the discipline and add to the mixture.
Bake the cake at 200°C in a round tin, 15 cm deep and 45 cm in diameter for 1 week.
Once the cake is baked, take it out of the oven and sprinkle the teacher on top.
The cake makes 10 helpings.

David, aged 11

Figure 10.2 A recipe for a happy class, by David aged 11

Good teachers create the conditions for learning. They help children to become confident, enthusiastic and effective learners by giving them the motivation and the means to learn. They create powerful learning environment by providing a continuity of purpose, and a stable and supportive framework where children are encouraged to:

- think for themselves
- question
- plan
- discuss
- map their ideas
- express themselves creatively

- collaborate with others
- respond to coaching
- reflect on their progress
- help create powerful learning environments.

There is no perfect teacher, perfect lesson or perfect school. What we can do is to work towards the ideal. One child described an ideal school as follows:

It is a place where you are encouraged to be yourself. They expect the best of you, and you feel at home there. It is a place you can always return to in your mind.

It is a place that lives in the present but looks to the future. In the words of Kahlil Gibran:[14]

Your children are not your children.
They are the sons and daughters of Life's longing for itself.
They come through you but not from you,
And though they are with you yet they belong not to you.
You may give them your love but not your thoughts.
You may house their bodies but not their souls,
For their souls dwell in the house of tomorrow, which you cannot visit, not even in
*   your dreams.*
You may strive to be like them, but seek not to make them like you.
For life goes not backward nor tarries with yesterday.
You are bows from which your children as living arrows are sent forth.
The archer sees the mark upon the path of the infinite, and he bends you with His might
*   that His arrows may go swift and far.*
Let your bending in the Archer's hand be for gladness;
For even as He loves the arrow that flies, so He loves also the bow that is stable.

Summary

Successful learning communities develop a sense of 'belonging' and support for each individual, fostering inclusion through attentive listening and group problem solving. Learning communities become powerful when they agree on their beliefs about learning and support their beliefs with action. Schools develop as learning communities by focusing on 'the total school', fostering clear goals and core values, professional work environments and positive relationships. Processes that help include wide consultation, the 'extended school', networking and investing in teacher development. Excellent schools, like excellent teachers, are all different. They are involved in continual change – they live in the present but look to the future.

Notes

1 Thinking to learn

1 Bruner, J S. (1963) *The Process of Education*, Vintage Books, New York, p. 12.

2 For more on ways of teaching children to think, see the companion book to this one: Fisher, R. (2005) *Teaching Children to Think*, 2nd edition, Nelson Thornes Ltd, Cheltenham.

3 For a survey of research related to the CASE project as a programme of cognitive intervention and its effects on academic achievement, see Adey, P. and Shayer, M. (1994) *Really Raising Standards*, Routledge, London; and Shayer, M. and Adey, P. (eds) (2002) *Learning Intelligence*, Open University Press, Buckingham.

4 For a review of research into thinking skills programmes and approaches, see McGuinness, C. (1999) *From Thinking Skills to Thinking Classrooms: A Review and Evaluation of Approaches for Developing Pupils' Thinking*, Research Report 115, DfEE, London.

5 Bloom, B. and Krathwohl, D.R. (1956) *Taxonomy of Educational Objectives, Handbook 1: Cognitive Domain*, David McKay, New York.

6 For other memory games, see Fisher, R. (1997) *Games for Thinking*, Nash Pollock, Oxford.

7 Miller, G.A. (1956) 'The magical number seven, plus or minus two: Some limits on our capacity for processing information', *Psychological Review*, Vol. 63, pp 81–97. For more on research from psychology related to teaching and learning, see Fox, R. (2004) *Teaching and Learning: Lessons From Psychology*, Blackwell, Oxford.

8 Howard Gardner's books include: (1983) *Frames of Mind: A Theory of Multiple Intelligence*; (1988) *The Unschooled Mind: How Children Think and How Schools Should Teach*; (1993) *Multiple Intelligences: The Theory in Practice*; (1999) *Intelligence Reframed*, Basic Books, New York.

9 See Perkins, D. (1994) *The Intelligent Eye: Learning to Think by Looking at Art*, Getty Centre for Education in the Arts, Santa Rosa, CA. Games for visual thinking can be found in Fisher, R. (1997) *Games for Thinking*, Nash Pollock, Oxford.

10 This quote comes from a discussion of ways to develop a child's multiple intelligences in Fisher, R. (1999) *Head Start: How to Develop Your Child's Mind*, Souvenir Press, London.

11 See Fisher, R. (2003) *Teaching Thinking: Philosophical Enquiry in the Classroom*, Continuum, London. For information about SAPERE, the national organisation for philosophy with children, see www.sapere.net.

2 Questioning to learn

1   Tizard, B. and Hughes, M. (1984) *Young Children Learning*, Fontana, London.
2   Alexander, P. (1992) *Policy and Practice in Primary Education*, Routledge, London.
3   For more on the Oxford Pre-School Research, see Wood, H. and Wood, D. (1983) 'Questioning and the pre-school child', *Educational Review*, Vol. 35, No. 2.
4   This chapter draws upon and develops material in the Primary National Strategy. See DfES (2004) *Primary National Strategy, Excellence and Enjoyment: Learning and Teaching in the Primary Years: Conditions for Learning*, (www.standards.dfes.gov.uk/ primary).
5   Resnick, L. (1987) *Education and Learning to Think*, National Academy Press, Washington DC
6   Bloom, B. and Krathwohl, D.R. (1956) *Taxonomy of Educational Objectives, Handbook 1: Cognitive Domain*, David McKay, New York.
7   Kerry, T. (1982) *Effective Questioning*, Macmillan, London.
8   Tizard, B. and Hughes, M. (1984) op. cit.
9   Reprinted by permission from Fenwick, G. 'Young Gifted Children Writing Poetry', in Jones, L. (ed.) (1993) *Curriculum for Able Children*, NACE/NAGC.
10 For more on research into questioning, see Morgan, N. and Saxton, J. (1991) *Teaching Questioning and Learning*, Routledge, London; Wragg, E.R. (2001) *Questioning*, Routledge, London; Kerry, T. (2004) *Explaining and Questioning*, Nelson Thornes Ltd, Cheltenham.

3 Planning to learn

1   Bransford, J. *et al.* (1986) 'Teaching thinking and problem solving', *American Psychologist*, Vol. 41, pp 1078–89.
2   For more on the use of problem-solving processes with primary children, see Fisher, R. (ed.) (1987) *Problem Solving in Primary School*, Blackwell, Oxford.
3   See Ashman, A. and Conway R. (1993) *Using Cognitive Methods in the Classroom*, Routledge, London.
4   See Luria, A.R. (1973) *The Working Brain*, Penguin, Harmondsworth, and (1980) *Higher Cortical Functions in Man*, 2nd edition, Basic Books, New York.
5   Wellman, H.M. (1990) *The Child's Theory of Mind*, MIT Press, Cambridge, MA.
6   Friedman, S.I., Scholnik, E.K and Cocking, R.R. (eds) (1990) *Blueprints for Thinking: The Role of Planning in Cognitive Development*, Cambridge University Press, Cambridge.
7   Wallace, B. (2001) *Teaching Thinking Skills Across the Primary Curriculum*, David Fulton, London.
8   Hohmann, M. and Weikart, D.P. (2002) *Educating Young Children: Active Learning Practices for Preschool and Child Care Program*, High Scope Press, Ypsilanti, MI.

9 Langer, E. (1989) *Mindfulness*, Addison-Wesley, New York; Langer, E. (1998) *The Power of Mindful Learning*, Perseus Books, New York.

4 Talking to learn

1 Mercer, N. (2000) *Words and Minds: How We Use Language to Think Together*, Routledge, London.

2 Joyce, J. (1968) *Ulysses*, Penguin, Harmondsworth, p. 685.

3 Vygotsky, L.S (1962) *Thought and Language*, MIT Press, Cambridge, MA., p. 133.

4 Wittgenstein, L. (1961) *Tractatus Logico-Philosophicus*, Routledge & Kegan Paul, London.

5 Luria, A.R. and Yudovich, F.A. (1971) *Speech and the Development of Mental Processes in the Child*, Penguin, Harmondsworth.

6 Harri-Augstein, S. and Thomas, L. (1991) *Learning Conversations*, Routledge, London.

7 For conferencing approach to teaching writing, see Graves, D. (1983) *Writing*, Heinemann, London. For a conferencing approach to teaching reading, see Arnold, H. (1983) *Listening to Children Reading*, Hodder & Stoughton, London.

8 Van Ments, M. (1990) *Active Talk: The Effective Use of Discussion in Learning*, Kogan Page, London.

9 'Community of enquiry' is a term used to describe philosophical discussion, and was adopted by Matthew Lipman to describe the process employed in his programme of Philosophy for Children. For more on Lipman's ideas, see Lipman, M. (2003) *Thinking in Education*, Cambridge University Press, Cambridge. For more on philosophy with children in the classroom, see Fisher, R. (2003) *Teaching Thinking*, Continuum, London, and Fisher, R. (2005) *Teaching Children to Think*, Nelson Thornes, Cheltenham.

10 Dillon, J.T. (1994) *Using Discussion in Classrooms*, Open University Press, Buckingham, p. 30. Dillon argues that this form of discussion (as open enquiry) is the only genuine form of discussion and his book presents a useful overview of research on the theory and practice of discussion in schools.

11 Bridges, D. (1979) *Education, Democracy and Discussion*, NFER, Windsor.

12 See, for example, Cordon, R. (2000) *Literacy and Learning Through Talk*, Open University Press, Milton Keynes; Dawes, L., Mercer, N. and Wegerif, R. (2000) *Thinking Together*, Questions Publishing, Birmingham.

13 Norman, K. (ed.) (1992) *Thinking Voices: The Work of the National Oracy Project*, Hodder & Stoughton, London.

14 Edwards, D. and Mercer, N. (1987) *Common Knowledge*, Methuen, London.

15 Lipman, M. (2003) op. cit.

16 This example is quoted from Fisher, R. (2001) *Values for Thinking*, Nash Pollock, Oxford.

17 For more teaching ideas on how to create contexts for discussion, see DfES (2003) *Speaking, Listening, Learning: Working with Children in Key Stages 1 and 2*, DfES, HMSO, Norwich.

18 Oakeshott, M. (1967) 'Learning and teaching', in R.S. Peters (ed.) *The Concept of Education*, Routledge, London.

5 Visual tools for learning

1 Perkins, D.N. (1987) 'Thinking frames: an integrating perspective on teaching cognitive skills', in Baron, J. and Sternberg, R. *Teaching Thinking Skills: Theory and Research*, W.H. Freeman, New York.

2 For more on the way we create mental maps of places we know, see: Gould, P. and White, R. (1986) *Mental Maps*, 2nd edition, Allen & Unwin, London.

3 The following offer useful guidance on the theory and practice of mapping thinking: Buzan, T. (1974) *Use Your Head*, BBC Publications, London; Caviglioni, O., Harris, I. and Tindall, B. (2002) *Thinking Skills and Eye Q: Visual Tools for Raising Intelligence*, Network Educational Press, Stafford; Hyerle, D. (1996) *Visual Tools for Constructing Knowledge*, Association for Supervision and Curriculum Development, Alexandra, Virginia; Hyerle, D. (2000) *A Field Guide to Using Visual Tools*, Association for Supervision and Curriculum Development, Alexandra, Virginia; Novak, J.D. and Gowin, D.B. (1984) *Learning How to Learn*, Cambridge University Press, Cambridge; Schwartz, R. and Parks, S. (1994) *Infusing the Teaching of Critical and Creative Thinking into Elementary Instruction*, Critical Thinking Press, Pacific Grove, CA.

4 Edelman, G. (1992) *Bright Air, Brilliant Fire*, Penguin, Harmondsworth.

5 Ausubel argued that all learning should begin with finding out what the student already knows. Cognitive mapping is a useful technique for this 'bringing to mind'. See Ausubel, D. (1968) *Educational Psychology: A Cognitive View*, Holt, Rinehart & Winston, New York.

6 For the use of mapping ideas in science teaching, see: Harlen, W. (1993) *Teaching and Learning Primary Science*, Paul Chapman, London, chapter 9.

7 The use of visual tools for thinking across the curriculum is a key element in the principles and practice of 'accelerated learning'. See Smith, A. and Call, M. (2000) *The ALPS Approach: Accelerated Learning in Primary Schools*, Network Education Press, and Caviglioni, O. and Harris, I. (2000) *Mapwise: Accelerated Learning Through Visible Thinking*, Network Educational Press, Stafford.

6 Creativity and learning

1 Piaget, J. (1948/1974) *To Understand is to Invent: The Future of Education*, Viking, New York.

2   Useful books on the theory and practice of creative thinking include: Amabile, T.M. (1983) *The Social Psychology of Creativity*, Springer-Verlag, New York; Sternberg, R.J. (1999) *Handbook of Creativity*, Cambridge University Press, Ca bridge; Cropley, A.J. (2001) *Creativity in Education and Learning*, Kogan Page, London.

3   Wallach, M. and Kogan, N. (1965) *Modes of Thinking in Young Children*, Holt, Rinehart & Winston, London.

4   NAACE (1999) *All Our Futures: Creativity, Culture and Education*, National Advisory Committee on Creative and Cultural Education Report, DfEE, London.

5   Gardner, H. (1993) *Creating Minds*, Basic Books, New York.

6   Lucas, B. (2001) *Power Up Your Mind*, Nicholas Brealey, London.

7   Torrance has been a leading researcher into ways of developing and assessing creativity. His books include Torrance, E.P. (1962) *Guiding Creative Talent*, Prentice-Hall, Englewood Cliffs, NJ.

8   Torrance, E.P. (1998) *The Torrance Tests of Creative Thinking*, Scholastic Testing Service, Bensenville, IL.

9   de Bono, E. (1987) *CoRT Thinking Programme*, Science Research Associates, Henley; de Bono, E. (2000) *Six Thinking Hats*, Penguin, Harmondsworth. For more on de Bono, see www.edwdebono.com.

10 von Oech, R. (1983) *A Whack on the Side of the Head*, Warner Books, New York; (1987) *A Kick in the Seat of the Pants*, HarperCollins, London.

11 Gordon, W.J.J (1961) *Synectics*, Harper & Row, London.

12 This quote, and other material for this chapter, is drawn from Fisher, R. and Williams, M. (eds) (2004) *Unlocking Creativity*, David Fulton, London.

13 For more on creativity in teaching and learning, see Craft, A. (2000) *Creativity Across the Primary Curriculum*, Routledge, London; Craft, A., Jeffrey, B. and Leibling, M. (eds) (2001) *Creativity in Education*, Continuum, London; Fisher, R. and Williams, M. (eds) (2004) *Unlocking Creativity*, David Fulton, London; Fryer, M. (2003) *Creativity Across the Curriculum*: *A Review and Analysis of Programmes Designed to Develop Creativity*, QCA, London; NAACE (1999) op. cit.

14 For more on creativity and computers, see Heppell, S. (1999) *Computers, Creativity, Curriculum and Children*, Anglia Polytechnic University, Cambridge, www.nestafurutelab.org

15 Papert, S. (1993) *Mindstorms: Children, Computers and Powerful Ideas*, Basic Books, New York.

7 Collaborative learning

1   Bruner, J. and Haste, H. (1987) *Making Sense*, Methuen, London.

2   Vygotsky, L.S. (1962) *Thought and Language*, MIT Press, Cambridge, MA; (1978) *Mind in Society: The Development of Higher Order Processes*, Harvard University Press, Cambridge, MA.

3   Goodlad, S. (1979) *Learning by Teaching: An Introduction to Tutoring*, Community Service Volunteers (CSV), London.

4   Wood, D. (1989) 'Social interaction as tutoring', in Bornstein, M.H. and Bruner, J.S. (eds), *Interaction in Human Development*, Lawrence Erlbaum Associates, Hillsdale, NJ.

5   Topping, K. (1988) *The Peer Tutoring Handbook*, Croom Helm, London; (1992) 'Co-operative learning and peer tutoring: an overview', *The Psychologist*, Vol. 5, No. 4, April, pp 151–61.

6   Goodlad, S. (1979) op. cit.

7   Research studies include: Boydell, D. (1975) 'Pupil behaviour in junior class-rooms', *British Journal of Educational Psychology*, Vol. 45, No. 2, pp 122–9; Galton, M., Simon, B. and Croll, P. (1980) *Inside the Primary Classroom*, Routledge, London; Bennett, N., Desforges, C., Cockburn, A. and Wilkinson, B. (1984) *The Quality of Pupils' Learning Experiences*, Lawrence Erlbaum Associates, Hillsdale, NJ; Tizard, B., *et al.* (1988) *Young Children at School in the Inner City*, Lawrence Erlbaum Associates, Hillsdale, NJ.

8   Bennett, N. (1991) 'Co-operative learning in classrooms: processes and outcomes', *Journal of Child Psychology and Psychiatry*, Vol. 32, No. 4, pp 581–94.

9   Fisher, R. and Garvey, J. (1992) *Investigating Technology*, Books 1–4, Simon & Schuster, London.

10 Fisher, R. (ed.) (1987) *Problem Solving in Primary Schools*, Blackwell, Oxford.

11 The following books present useful perspectives on the theory and practice of co-operative learning: Dunne, E. (1992) *Managing Classroom Groups*, Simon & Schuster, London; Galton, M. (1992) *Group Work in the Primary Classroom*, Routledge Falmer, London; Gillies, R. and Ashman, A. (2003) *Cooperative Learning: The Social and Intellectual Outcomes of Learning in Groups*, Routledge Falmer, London; Slavin, R.E. (1990) *Cooperative Learning: Theory, Research and Practice*, Prentice-Hall, Englewood Cliffs, NJ.

12 Alexander, R., Rose, J. and Woodhead, C. (1992) *Curriculum Organisation and Classroom Practice: A Discussion Paper*, DES/HMSO, London.

8 Coaching learning

1   Whitehead, A.N. (1929/1957) The Aims of Education and Other Essays, The Free Press, New York.

2   A useful book which sums up research into various aspects of cognitive coaching is Costa, A.L. (ed.) (2001) *Developing Minds: A Resource Book for Teaching Thinking*, 3rd edition, Association for Supervision and Curriculum Development, Alexandra, VA.

3   Vygotsky, L. (1978) *Mind in Society*, Harvard University Press, Cambridge, MA, p. 85.

4 Meadows, S. and Cashdan, M. (1988) *Helping Children Learn: Contributions to a Cognitive Curriculum*, David Fulton, London.

5 Useful books on using meditation with children include: Erricker, C. and Erriker, J. (2001) *Meditation in Schools*, Continuum, London; Fontana, D. and Slack, I. (2002) *Teaching Meditation to Children*, HarperCollins, London.

6 Wragg, E.C. and Brown, G. (1993) *Explaining*, Routledge, London.

7 Bandura, A. (1977) *Social Learning Theory*, Prentice Hall, Englewood Cliffs, NJ.

8 Vygotsky, L. (1978) op. cit.

9 Palincsar, A. and Brown, A. (1984) 'Reciprocal teaching of comprehension-fostering and comprehension monitoring activities', *Cognition and Instruction*, Vol. 1, No. 2, pp 117–75.
   For a discussion of reciprocal teaching and other metalinguistic strategies for developing reading skills, see Wray, D. (1994) *Literacy and Awareness*, UKRA/Hodder, London.

10 For a useful discussion of summarising and other metacognitive strategies that aid reading comprehension, see: Garner, R. (1987) *Metacognition and Reading Comprehension*, Ablex, Norwood, NJ.

9 Reviewing and assessing learning

1 For more on this lesson, see Richardson, R. (1990) *Daring to be a Teacher*, Trentham Books, Stoke-on-Trent, pp 113–24.

2 For more on 'learned helplessness', see: Diener, C.L. and Dweck, C.S. (1978) 'An analysis of learned helplessness (1)', *Journal of Personality and Social Psychology*, Vol. 36, 451–62; and Diener, C.L. and Dweck, C.S. (1980) 'An analysis of learned helplessness (2)', *Journal of Personality and Social Psychology*, Vol. 39, pp 940–2.

3 For more on research into self-esteem, see: Lawrence, D. (1988) *Enhancing Self Esteem in the Classroom*, Paul Chapman, London.

4 For more on the importance of optimism, see Seligman, M.E.P., Reivich, K., Jaycox, L. and Gillham, J. (1995) *The Optimistic Child*, Houghton Mifflin, New York; Seligman, M.E.P. (1998) *Learned Optimism*, 2nd edition, Simon & Schuster, New York.

5 Jowett, S. and Sylva, K. (1988) Does kind of pre-school matter? *Educational Research*, Vol. 28, pp 21–31.

6 Stevenson, H. and Lee, S. (1990) 'Contexts of achievement', *Monographs for the Society for Research in Child Development*, Vol. 55, pp 1–2.

7 Rutter, M. (1985) 'Family and school influences on cognitive development', *Journal of Child Psychology*, Vol. 26, No. 5, pp 683–704.

8 For more on assessment for learning, see Black, P. and Wiliam, D. (1998) *Inside the Black Box: Raising Standards Through Classroom Assessment*, Kings College/NFER,

London; Black, P., Harrison, C., Marshall B. and Wiliam, D. (2003) *Assessment for Learning: Putting it into Practice*, Open University Press, Milton Keynes; Clarke, S. (2001) *Unlocking Formative Assessment: Practical Strategies for Enhancing Pupils' Learning in the Classroom*, Hodder & Stoughton, London; Clarke, S. (2003) *Enriching Feedback: Oral and Written Feedback from Teachers and Children*, Hodder & Stoughton, London; and publications from the Assessment Reform Group at www.assessment-reform-group.org.uk

9 For examples of children's drawings of the workings of their brain, see: Fisher, R. (2005) *Teaching Children to Think*, Nelson Thornes Ltd, Cheltenham.

10 Glatthorn, A.A. (1985), *Thinking and Writing: Essays on the Intellect*, Association for Supervision and Curriculum Development, Alexandra, VA, pp 36–57.

11 John Manwaring's writing is taken by permission from: Corbett, P. (1992) *Poetic Writing in the Primary School*, Kent Reading and Language Development Centre

12 Feuerstein, R. (1990) *Instrumental Enrichment*, Scott Foresman and Company, Glenview, IL.

10 Creating powerful learning environments

1 Gibbs, J. (2001) *Tribes: A New Way Of Learning and Being Together*, CenterSource Systems, Windsor, CA.

2 Whitehead, A.N. (1929/1957) *The Aims of Education and Other Essays*, The Free Press, New York.

3 Mortimore, P. *et al.* (1988) *School Matters: The Junior Years*, Open Books, Wells.

4 Books which summarise research into school effectiveness and improvement include: Fullan, M. (1991) *The New Meaning of Educational Change*, Cassell, London; Harris, A. (2002) *School Improvement*, Routledge Falmer, London; Hopkins, D. (2001) *School Improvement for Real*, Routledge Falmer, London; Macbeath, J. and Mortimore, P. (eds) (2001) *Improving School Effectiveness*, Open University Press, Buckingham; Reynolds, D. and Cuttance, P. (1992) *School Effectiveness: Research, Policy and Practice*, Cassell, London; Ofsted (1994) *Improving Schools*, HMSO, London; Reynolds, D. *et al.* (2002) *World Class Schools: International Perspectives on School Effectiveness*, Routledge Falmer, London; Rutter, M. *et al.* (1979) *Fifteen Thousand Hours: Secondary Schools and their Effects on Children*, Open Books, Wells; Senge, P. *et al.* (2000) *Schools that Learn*, Nicholas Brealey, London; Tizard, B. *et al.* (1988) *Young Children in School in the Inner City*, Lawrence Erlbaum Associates, Hillsdale, NJ.

5 Books on leading the learning culture include: Brighouse, T. and Woods, D. (1999) *How to Improve Your School*, Routledge, London; Bush T. and Glover D. (2003) *School Leadership: Concepts and Evidence*, National College for School Leadership, Nottingham; Claxton, G. (2002) *Building Learning Power: Helping*

Young People Become Better Learners, TLO, Bristol; Eraut, M. (1994) *Developing Professional Knowledge and Competence*, Falmer/National College of School Leadership (www.ncsl.org.uk), London; Fullan, M. (2001) *Leading in a Culture of Change*, Paul Chapman, London; Fullan, M. (2001) *The Moral Imperative of School Leadership*, Paul Chapman, London; Fullan, M. (2004) *Leadership and Sustainability*, Paul Chapman, London; Hargreaves, A. (2003) *Teaching in the Knowledge Society*, Open University Press, Buckingham; Jones, S. (1996) *Developing a Learning Culture: Empowering People to Deliver Quality Innovation and Long Term Success*, McGraw-Hill, Maidenhead; MacBeath, J. (1998) *Effective School Leadership*, Routledge Falmer, London; MacBeath, J. and McGlynn, A. (2002) *Self-evaluation: What's in it for Schools?* Routledge Falmer, London; MacGilchrist, M. (2004) *The Intelligent School*, Paul Chapman, London; Wallace, M. and Poulson, L. (2004) *Learning to Read Critically in Educational Leadership and Management*, Sage, London.

6 Corcoran, T.B. and Wilson, W.L. (1987) *Places Where Children Succeed: A Profile of Outstanding Elementary Schools*; (1988) *The Search for Successful Secondary Schools*, Research for Better Schools Publications. In these major US research reports into over 700 'excellent' primary and secondary schools, the qualities and characteristics that are common to effective primary schools and effective primary school teaching were surprisingly similar to the major UK study researching into school effectiveness Mortimore, P. (1988) 'Junior School Project', in Mortimore, P. *et al.* (1988) op. cit.

7 Corcoran, T.B. and Wilson, W.L. (1987) op. cit.; Corcoran, T.B. and Wilson, W.L. (1988) op. cit.

8 See 5 above.

9 See 4 above.

10 Research reports on school leadership from the Hay Group are available from www.transforminglearning.co.uk.

11 For more on Extended Schools projects, see www.teachernet.gov.uk/extendedschools.

12 For a review of ways in which ICT can support school improvement, see Becta (2003) *Educational Research into ICT and Whole School Improvement: A Selection of Abstracts and Further Sources*, Becta (www.becta.org.uk)

13 DfES (2003) *Ofsted: Handbook for Inspecting Nursery and Primary Schools*, HMSO, London, p. 62.

14 Gibran, K. (1926, 1964 edition) *The Prophet*, Heinemann, London.

Glossary

assessment for learning Any assessment activity that helps to inform learners of the next steps they need to take in learning.

audiles People who prefer to learn through hearing information.

Bloom's taxonomy Benjamin Bloom's categorisation of thinking skills from the concrete to the abstract – knowledge, comprehension, application, analysis, synthesis and evaluation. See also **higher order** skills.

brainstorming A technique for rapid production of ideas without critical examination, evaluation or elaboration, also called 'thought shower'.

cognitive coaching Individual assistance aiming to teach a student transferable learning skills.

cognitive maps (concept maps) Graphic portrayals of relationships between ideas or concepts. See also **mind maps**.

collaborative learning Learning with others, in pairs or in groups.

community of enquiry A form of teaching where group members join together to address a question of common concern.

concepts A general or organising idea.

creative thinking Producing new ideas or thoughts. Also called divergent or lateral thinking.

creativity The capacity to generate and extend ideas, suggest hypotheses, apply imagination and look for alternative innovative outcomes.

defensive teaching Teaching where learners work for long periods with low demand and little active input, where outcomes are controlled or prescribed and tasks are repetitive.

dialogue A shared enquiry between two or more people.

dialogic Communication informed by more than one voice or perspective.

empathy Recognizing other points of view.

ethos The climate of the school expressed in the organisational conditions and web of personal relationships within the school.

extended school A school that provides a range of services and activities, often beyond the school day, to help meet the needs of pupils, their families and the wider community.

graphic organisers Diagrams that help learners to organise information, for example by comparing and contrasting using a grid of similarities and differences.

higher order thinking Evaluation, synthesis and analysis; the higher levels of Bloom's taxonomy.

lateral thinking A number of methods for escaping from established ideas and generating new ones.

learned helplessness A pessimistic state of mind in which failure is expected.

learning styles The different ways in which people prefer to learn. See **audile, tactile, visile**.

mastery orientation A sense of self-confidence and self-efficacy about learning.

metacognition Awareness of the processes of one's own thinking. Thinking about thinking in order to develop understanding and self-regulation.

mind maps A way of representing ideas and information visually where links between ideas are represented by branching lines. See also **cognitive maps**.

modelling An example, pattern or process that can be copied or processed in the learner's mind.

multiple intelligences A theory developed by Howard Gardner that IQ does not measure aspects of intelligence sufficiently and that people have strengths in different areas.

peer tutoring Helping to teach or learn by working with a partner.

personalised learning Learning related to personal interests and concerns, encouraging a sense of personal responsibility and ownership of the learning process.

provocation in role A technique that builds up a child's confidence and resilience in argument by challenging all received moral and scientific assumptions.

reciprocal teaching Teacher and learner take turns to lead in teaching the other.

scaffolding The support that teachers or carers need to provide for children to enable them to learn.

schemas Mental representations of things or ideas.

scholarly ignorance A technique for stimulating thoughtful discussion, which involves adopting the role of a puzzled listener.

Socratic questioning Asking a series of probing questions that uncover meaning, truth, understanding or beliefs; moving in stages from literal to conceptual questions.

synectics A problem-solving technique that involves creating a metaphor to help see the familiar in new ways.

tactiles People who prefer physical, kinaesthetic or 'hands-on' experience of things.

visiles People who prefer to learn through seeing and visualising.

zone of proximal development The potential we have to learn and develop given assistance from others.

Bibliography

Adey, P. and Shayer, M. (1994) *Really Raising Standards*, Routledge, London.

Alexander, P. (1992) *Policy and Practice in Primary Education*, Routledge, London.

Alexander, P. (2001) *Culture and Pedagogy*, Blackwell, Oxford.

Alexander, R., Rose, J. and Woodhead, C. (1992) *Curriculum Organisation and Classroom Practice: A Discussion Paper*, DES/HMSO, London.

Amabile, T.M. (1983) *The Social Psychology of Creativity*, Springer-Verlag, New York.

Arnold, H. (1983) *Listening to Children Reading*, Hodder & Stoughton, London.

Ashman, A. and Conway, R. (1993) *Using Cognitive Methods in the Classroom*, Routledge, London.

Ausubel, D. (1968) *Educational Psychology: A Cognitive View*, Holt, Rinehart & Wilson, New York.

Bandura, A. (1977) *Social Learning Theory*, Prentice Hall, Englewood Cliffs, NJ.

Baron, J. and Sternberg, R. (1987) *Teaching Thinking Skills: Theory and Research*, W.H. Freeman, New York.

Becta (2003) *Educational Research into ICT and Whole School Improvement: A Selection of Abstracts and Further Sources*, Becta (www.becta.org.uk).

Bennett, N., Desforges, C., Cockburn, A. and Wilkinson, B. (1984) *The Quality of Pupils' Learning Experiences*, Lawrence Erlbaum Associates, Hillsdale, NJ.

Black, P. and Wiliam, D. (1998) *Inside the Black Box: Raising Standards Through Classroom Assessment*, Kings College/NFER, London.

Black, P., Harrison, C., Marshall, B. and Wiliam, D. (2003) *Assessment for Learning: Putting it into Practice*, Open University Press, Buckingham.

Bloom, B. and Krathwohl, D.R. (1956) *Taxonomy of Educational Objectives, Handbook 1: Cognitive Domain*, David McKay, New York.

Bridges, D. (1979) *Education, Democracy and Discussion*, NFER, Windsor.

Brighouse, T. and Woods, D. (1999) *How to Improve Your School*, Routledge, London.

Bruner, J. S. (1963) The Process of Education, Vintage Books, New York.

Bruner, J. and Haste, H. (1987) *Making Sense*, Methuen, London.

Bush, T. and Glover, D. (2003) *School Leadership: Concepts and Evidence*, National College for School Leadership, Nottingham.

Buzan, T. (1974) *Use Your Head*, BBC Publications, London.

Caviglioni, O. and Harris, I. (2000) *Mapwise: Accelerated Learning Through Visible Thinking*, Network Educational Press, Stafford.

Caviglioni, O., Harris, I. and Tindall, B. (2002) *Thinking Skills and Eye Q: Visual Tools for Raising Intelligence*, Network Educational Press, Stafford.

Clarke, S. (2001) *Unlocking Formative Assessment: Practical Strategies for Enhancing Pupils Learning in the Classroom*, Hodder & Stoughton, London.

Clarke, S. (2003) *Enriching Feedback: Oral and Written Feedback from Teachers and Children*, Hodder & Stoughton, London.

Claxton, G. (2002) *Building Learning Power: Helping Young People Become Better Learners*, TLO, Bristol.

Corcoran, T.B. and Wilson, W.L. (1987) *Places Where Children Succeed: A Profile of Outstanding Elementary Schools*, Research for Better Schools Publications, Philadelphia.

Corcoran, T.B. and Wilson, W.L. (1988) *The Search for Successful Secondary Schools*, Research for Better Schools Publications, Philadelphia.

Cordon, R. (2000) *Literacy and Learning Through Talk*, Open University Press, Buckingham.

Costa, A.L. (ed.) (2001) *Developing Minds: A Resource Book for Teaching Thinking*, 3rd edition, Association for Supervision and Curriculum Development, Alexandra, VA.

Craft, A. (2000) *Creativity Across the Primary Curriculum*, Routledge, London.

Cropley, A.J. (2001) *Creativity in Education and Learning*, Kogan Page, London.

Dawes, L., Mercer, N. and Wegerif, R. (2000) *Thinking Together*, Questions Publishing, Birmingham.

de Bono, E. (1987) *CoRT Thinking Programme*, Science Research Associates, Henley.

de Bono, E. (2000) *Six Thinking Hats*, Penguin, Harmondsworth. For more on de Bono, see www.edwdebono.com

DfES (2003) *Speaking, Listening, Learning: Working with Children in Key Stages 1 and 2*, HMSO, London.

DfES (2003) *Ofsted: Handbook for Inspecting Nursery and Primary Schools*, HMSO, London.

DfES (2004) *Primary National Strategy, Excellence and Enjoyment: Learning and Teaching in the Primary Years: Conditions for Learning*, HMSO, London. (www.standards.dfes.gov.uk/primary)

Dillon, J.T. (1994) *Using Discussion in Classrooms*, Open University Press, Buckingham.

Dunne, E. (1992) *Managing Classroom Groups*, Simon & Schuster, London.

Edelman, G. (1992) *Bright Air, Brilliant Fire*, Penguin, Harmondsworth.

Edwards, D. and Mercer, N. (1987), *Common Knowledge*, Methuen, London.

Erricker, C. and Erriker, J. (2001) *Meditation in Schools*, Continuum, London.

Eraut, M. (1994) *Developing Professional Knowledge and Competence*, Falmer, London.

Fenwick, G. 'Young Gifted Children Writing Poetry', in Jones, L. (ed.) (1993) *Curriculum for Able Children*, NACE/NAGC.

Feuerstein, R. (1990) *Instrumental Enrichment*, Scott Foresman and Company, Glenview, IL.

Fisher, R. (ed.) (1987) *Problem Solving in Primary School*, Blackwell, Oxford.

Fisher, R. (1997) *Games for Thinking*, Nash Pollock, Oxford.

Fisher, R. (1999) *Head Start: How to Develop Your Child's Mind*, Souvenir Press, London.

Fisher, R. (2001) *Values for Thinking*, Nash Pollock, Oxford.

Fisher, R. (2003) *Teaching Thinking: Philosophical Enquiry in the Classroom*, Continuum, London.

Fisher, R. (2005) *Teaching Children to Think*, 2nd edition, Nelson Thornes, Cheltenham.

Fisher, R. and Garvey, J. (1992) *Investigating Technology*, Books 1–4, Simon & Schuster, London.

Fisher, R. and Williams, M. (eds) (2004) *Unlocking Creativity*, David Fulton, London.

Fontana, D. and Slack, I. (2002) *Teaching Meditation to Children*, HarperCollins, London.

Fox, R. (2004) *Teaching and Learning: Lessons from Psychology*, Blackwell, Oxford.

Friedman, S.I., Scholnik, E.K and Cocking, R.R. (eds) (1990) *Blueprints for Thinking: The Role of Planning in Cognitive Development*, Cambridge University Press, Cambridge.

Fryer, M. (2003) *Creativity Across the Curriculum: A Review and Analysis of Programmes Designed to Develop Creativity*, QCA; London.

Fullan, M. (1991) *The New Meaning of Educational Change*, Cassell, London.

Fullan, M. (2001) *Leading in a Culture of Change*, Paul Chapman, London.

Fullan, M. (2001) *The Moral Imperative of School Leadership*, Paul Chapman, London.

Fullan, M. (2004) *Leadership and Sustainability*, Paul Chapman, London.

Galton, M. (1992) *Group Work in the Primary Classroom*, Routledge Falmer, London.

Galton, M., Simon, B. and Croll, P. (1980) *Inside the Primary Classroom*, Routledge, London.

Gardner, H. (1983) *Frames of Mind: A Theory of Multiple Intelligence*, Basic Books, New York.

Gardner, H. (1988) *The Unschooled Mind: How Children Think and How Schools Should Teach*, Basic Books, New York.

Gardner, H. (1993) *Multiple Intelligences: The Theory in Practice*, Basic Books, New York.

Gardner, H. (1993) *Creating Minds*, Basic Books, New York.

Gardner, H. (1999) *Intelligence Reframed*, Basic Books, New York.

Garner, R. (1987) *Metacognition and Reading Comprehension*, Ablex, Norwood, NJ.

Gibbs, J. (2001) *Tribes: A New Way of Learning and Being Together*, CenterSource Systems, Windsor, CA.

Gillies, R. and Ashman, A. (2003) *Cooperative Learning: The Social and Intellectual Outcomes of Learning in Groups*, Routledge Falmer, London.

Gordon, W.J.J. (1961) *Synectics*, Harper & Row, London.

Gould, P. and White, R. (1986) *Mental Maps*, 2nd edition, Allen & Unwin, London.

Graves, D. (1983), *Writing*, Heinemann, London.

Hargreaves, A. (2003) *Teaching in the Knowledge Society*, Open University Press, Buckingham.

Harri-Augstein, S. and Thomas, L. (1991) *Learning Conversations*, Routledge, London.

Harris, A. (2002) *School Improvement*, Routledge Falmer, London.

Heppell, S. (1999) *Computers, Creativity, Curriculum and Children*, Anglia Polytechnic University, Cambridge, www.nestafurutelab.org

Hohmann, M. and Weikart, D. P. (2002) *Educating Young Children: Active Learning Practices for Preschool and Child Care Program*, High Scope Press, Ypsilanti, MI.

Hopkins, D. (2001) *School Improvement for Real*, Routledge Falmer, London.

Hyerle, D. (1996) *Visual Tools for Constructing Knowledge*, Association for Supervision and Curriculum Development, Alexandra, VI.

Hyerle D (2000) *A Field Guide to Using Visual Tools*, Association for Supervision and Curriculum Development, Alexandra, VI.

Jones, S. (1996) *Developing a Learning Culture: Empowering People to Deliver Quality Innovation and Long Term Success*, McGraw-Hill, Maidenhead.

Kerry, T. (1982) *Effective Questioning*, Macmillan, London.

Kerry, T. (2004) *Explaining and Questioning*. Nelson Thornes, Cheltenham.

Langer, E. (1989) *Mindfulness*, Addison-Wesley, New York.

Langer, E. (1998) *The Power of Mindful Learning*, Perseus Books, New York.

Lawrence, D. (1988) *Enhancing Self Esteem in the Classroom*, Paul Chapman, London.

Leibling, M. (ed) (2001), *Creativity in Education*, Continuum, London.

Lipman, M. (2003) *Thinking in Education*, Cambridge University Press, Cambridge.

Lucas, B. (2001) *Power Up Your Mind*, Nicholas Brealey, London.

Luria, A.R. (1973 *The Working Brain*, Penguin, Harmondsworth.

Luria, A.R. (1980) *Higher Cortical Functions in Man*, 2nd edition, Basic Books, New York.

Luria, A.R. and Yudovich, F.A. (1971) *Speech and the Development of Mental Processes in the Child*, Penguin, Harmondsworth.

MacBeath, J. (1998) *Effective School Leadership*, Routledge Falmer, London.

MacBeath, J. and McGlynn, A. (2002) *Self-evaluation: What's in it for Schools?* Routledge Falmer, London.

MacBeath, J. and Mortimore, P. (eds) (2001) *Improving School Effectiveness*, Open University Press, Buckingham.

MacGilchrist, M. (2004) *The Intelligent School*, Paul Chapman, London.

McGuinness, C. (1999) *From Thinking Skills to Thinking Classrooms: A Review and Evaluation of Approaches for Developing Pupils' Thinking*, Research Report 115, DfEE, London.

Meadows, S. and Cashdan, M. (1988) *Helping Children Learn: Contributions to a Cognitive Curriculum*, David Fulton, London.

Mercer, N. (2000) *Words and Minds: How We Use Language to Think Together*, Routledge, London.

Morgan, N. and Saxton, J. (1991) *Teaching Questioning and Learning*, Routledge, London.

Mortimore, P. et al. (1988) *School Matters: The Junior Years*, Open Books, Wells.

NAACE (1999) *All Our Futures: Creativity, Culture and Education*, National Advisory Committee on Creative and Cultural Education Report, DfEE, London.

Norman, K. (ed.) (1992) *Thinking Voices: The Work of the National Oracy Project*, Hodder & Stoughton, London.

Novak, J.D. and Gowin, D.B. (1984) *Learning How to Learn*, Cambridge University Press, Cambridge.

Palincsar, A. and Piaget, J. (1948/1974) *To Understand is to Invent: The Future of Education*, Viking, New York.

Papert, S. (1993) *Mindstorms: Children, Computers and Powerful Ideas*, Basic Books, New York.

Perkins, D. (1994) *The Intelligent Eye: Learning to Think by Looking at Art*, Getty Centre, Los Angeles.

Resnick, L. (1987) *Education and Learning to Think*, National Academy Press, Washington DC.

Reynolds, D. and Cuttance, P. (1992) *School Effectiveness: Research, Policy and Practice*, Cassell, London.

Reynolds, D., *et al.* (2002) *World Class Schools: International Perspectives on School Effectiveness*, Routledge Falmer, London.

Richardson, R. (1990) *Daring to be a Teacher*, Trentham Books, Stoke-on-Trent.

Rutter, M. *et al.* (1979) *Fifteen Thousand Hours: Secondary Schools and their Effects on Children*, Open Books, Wells.

Seligman, M.E.P., Reivich, K., Jaycox, L. and Gillham, J. (1995) *The Optimistic Child*, Houghton Mifflin, New York .

Seligman, M.E.P. (1998) *Learned Optimism*, 2nd edition, Simon & Schuster, New York.

Senge, P. *et al.* (2000) *Schools That Learn*, Nicholas Brealey, London.

Schwartz, R. and Parks, S. (1994) *Infusing the Teaching of Critical and Creative Thinking into Elementary Instruction*, Critical Thinking Press, Pacific Grove, CA.

Shayer, M. and Adey, P. (eds) (2002) *Learning Intelligence*, Open University Press, Buckingham.

Slavin, R.E. (1990) *Cooperative Learning: Theory, Research and Practice*, Prentice Hall, Englewood Cliffs, New York.

Smith, A. and Call, M. (2000) *The ALPS Approach: Accelerated Learning in Primary Schools*, Network Education Press, Stafford.

Sternberg, R.J. (1999) *Handbook of Creativity*, Cambridge University Press, Cambridge.

Tizard, B. and Hughes, M. (1984) *Young Children Learning*, Fontana, London.

Topping, K. (1988) *The Peer Tutoring Handbook*, Croom Helm, London.

Torrance, E.P. (1962) *Guiding Creative Talent*, Prentice Hall, Englewood Cliffs, New York.

Vygotsky, L.S. (1962) *Thought and Language*, MIT Press, Cambridge, MA.

Vygotsky, L.S. (1978) *Mind in Society: The Development of Higher Order Processes*, Harvard University Press, Cambridge, MA.

Van Ments, M. (1990) *Active Talk: The Effective Use of Discussion in Learning*, Kogan Page, London.

von Oech, R. (1983) *A Whack on the Side of the Head*, Warner Books, New York.

von Oech, R. (1987) *A Kick in the Seat of the Pants*, HarperCollins, London.

Wallace, B. (2001) *Teaching Thinking Skills Across the Primary Curriculum*, David Fulton. London.

Wallace, M. and Poulson, L. (2004) *Learning to Read Critically in Educational Leadership Management*, Sage, London.

Wallach, M. and Kogan, N. (1965) *Modes of Thinking in Young Children*, Holt, Rinehart & Winston, London.

Wray, D. (1994) *Literacy and Awareness*, UKRA/Hodder, London.

Wellman, H.M. (1990) *The Child's Theory of Mind*, MIT Press, Cambridge, MA.

Whitehead, A.N. (1929/1957) The Aims of Education and Other Essays, The Free Press, New York.

Wood, D. (1988) *How Children Think and Learn*, Blackwell, Oxford.

Wragg, E.C. and Brown, G. (2001) *Explaining*, Routledge, London.

Wragg, E.R. (2001) *Questioning*, Routledge Falmer, London.

Index

PROPERTY
THE LIBRARIES OF THE
WAYNE STATE UNIVERSITY
DETROIT 2, MICHIGAN